Whose life is it anyway ?

When to

Stop Taking Care of

THEIR FEELINGS &

Start Taking Care of

YOUR OWN

NINA W. BROWN, ED.D., LPC, NCC

New Harbinger Publications, Inc.

Publisher's Note

This publication is designed to provide accurate and authoritative information in regard to the subject matter covered. It is sold with the understanding that the publisher is not engaged in rendering psychological, financial, legal, or other professional services. If expert assistance or counseling is needed, the services of a competent professional should be sought.

Distributed in the U.S.A. by Publishers Group West; in Canada by Raincoast Books; in Great Britain by Airlift Book Company, Ltd.; in South Africa by Real Books, Ltd.; in Australia by Boobook; and in New Zealand by Tandem Press.

Cover design by Blue Design
Text design by Tracy Powell-Carlson

ISBN 1-57224-289-2 Paperback
All Rights Reserved
Printed in the United States of America

New Harbinger Publications' Web site address: www.newharbinger.com

04   03   02

10   9   8   7   6   5   4   3   2   1

First printing

This book is dedicated to the wonders and joy in my life: Billy, Joey, Samantha, Christopher, Nicholas, and Emma.

Contents

Acknowledgments

No book is produced in isolation. Many people, other than the author, contribute to the ideas, the creation and production, and their contributions should be recognized. It is not possible to include all the sources for the ideas in this book as many are embedded in my experiences, education, and work. The acknowledgments here are the clearly identifiable sources that had an impact on the production of this book.

Major sources of inspiration and education are the therapists and presentations at the Mid-Atlantic Group Psychotherapy Society and the American Group Psychotherapy Association. These knowledgeable and gifted therapists have given me a better understanding of the human condition.

There are specific individuals who provided me with encouragement and support and I wish to thank them. Fred Adair, my doctoral advisor; Bill Drewry and Jim Cross, my engineering friends; George Saiger, Joan Medway, Barry Bukatman, my colleagues at the Mid-Atlantic Group Psychotherapy Society; Rosemary Thompson, who is always a friend and colleague; and Wilford Brown, my husband.

Introduction

This book started out to address the concerns of people who feel they have too much empathy, and who want some new ideas about how not to get so caught up in others' feelings that they lose sight of their own values and needs. Even those who don't routinely get caught up in others' emotions can relate to this concern, as many people have experienced unwanted empathy with others at some point in their lives. As I reflected on how to address this topic, it seemed to me that what is most helpful for the overly empathic person is the protection of emotional shielding. Indeed, "Emotional Shielding" was the original title of the book.

As the book progressed the title changed, although the original thrust remained, that of emotional shielding. The main idea behind emotional shielding is that you can protect yourself from unwanted emotional assaults both from the outside world and from your inner world. When your empathy is triggered, that can also trigger unwanted feelings of guilt and shame, which, in turn, can lead you to doing things you do not wish to do.

Also central to this book is the understanding that we get more out of life if we have meaningful relationships and give of ourselves to others. If you were to consider only your own feelings important, you would soon find your relationships unsatisfactory, your life emotionally constricted, and you would be likely to be lonely and perhaps alienated. It is essential for our emotional and psychological well-being to reach out and make contact with others.

How to Use This Book

Nothing presented in this book is intended to suggest that you should only or always take care of your own feelings first. What is intended is that reading the discussions and doing the exercises will guide you to a clearer understanding of when your own needs and feelings should take precedence and when others' feelings should have top priority.

This balance between others' needs and your own is not easy to achieve, nor will you always be able to set priorities. Nevertheless, you can learn how to

- Reduce your family enmeshment

- Reduce your emotional susceptibility

- Begin to take care of yourself

- Do things for others because you *want* to, not because you were manipulated or intimidated

Constructive Changes

If you are feeling some long-term effects of family enmeshment and you are still taking care of others, you will want to think about how to make *constructive* changes. "Constructive" in the sense that you want to become independent instead of being enmeshed; however, you do not want to alienate family members nor do you want to become so self-absorbed that you become insensitive to others' needs and emotions.

What this book intends to do is to guide you to a better understanding of the following issues:

- Your emotional susceptibility and your family-of-origin behaviors that contribute to your emotional susceptibility

- How you are manipulated to take care of others when this may not be in your best interests

- How to create strategies that will help you to make constructive changes

- How to become more independent.

A lot of the material in this book is complex and interrelated. The subject is abstract, and much of what is presented and discussed cannot be objectively observed. Your feelings will be your guide. However, our feelings are not the most rational parts of ourselves, and they can be misleading. It would be helpful if you can allow yourself to read what is presented with an open mind, and not reject it immediately. Consider and reflect on everything you read with the attitude of, "What if it is accurate?"

A considerable amount of attention is given to personal growth and development, as they are fundamental to providing you with the resources you need to combat emotional contagion and emotional susceptibility. Such resources are also useful for learning how to build appropriate boundaries, the lack of which may be contributing to your manipulation by others. Your positive traits, such as openness and caring, are not neglected, as they are essential to forming satisfying relationships. Your intention should be to learn how to make constructive use of the positive aspects of openness and caring while, at the same time, warding off those aspects that may have left you vulnerable to manipulation by others.

The book also has various self-assessment exercises and activities for self-reflection. The self-assessment exercises are very informal and are focused on behaviors, attitudes, and feelings. Formal, more in-depth assessments and growth activities can be undertaken with the aid of a competent therapist. Readers are encouraged to use that means for deeper, more comprehensive understanding and personal life changes. The material here is intended to raise personal awareness and to provide some suggested short-term strategies that can bring relief.

Chapter 1

Overwhelmed, Enmeshed, and Manipulated

Barbara got a sinking feeling in her stomach when she heard the phone ring. Most days this was about the time her mother called, and Barbara feared that her mother had a new demand for her. Sure enough, the caller was her mother wanting Barbara to take her to the mall to buy some dishcloths. Barbara tried to say no, but she finally gave in and agreed to take her to the mall after the older woman whined that her children were all too busy to give her any of their time. Although Barbara knew this certainly wasn't the truth in her case (she saw her mother two or three times every week and talked with her on the phone almost every day), she heard the loneliness in her mother's voice and felt she had to give in.

John's law school graduation was to be celebrated the following day, but he was not happy or pleased. He knew that the day meant a lot to his parents. They had talked about his becoming a lawyer for as long as he could remember. Any indication on his part that he might seek another career had always been countered by his father stating, "It would break your mother's heart if you did not attend law school." John had capitulated and he will receive his law degree tomorrow. He has resolved, however, that now that he has fulfilled his parents' expectations for him, he will do what he has always wanted to do—become a policeman and try to make a career out of law enforcement.

Enmeshed Families

Both Barbara and John are experiencing *family enmeshment*. That means they give other people's feelings priority over their own. Because

Barbara and John have been conditioned to feel responsible for others' well-being, especially for their immediate family members, they are caught in a trap where they can be manipulated or intimidated into doing things they do not want to do, or things that may not be in their best interests.

Strong, healthy, nonenmeshed families allow family members to be independent, and their family dynamics cultivate *interdependence*. Family members share, cooperate, and are interested in each other's well-being, but they are also allowed to separate and to become unique individuals. For example, in a nonenmeshed family, Barbara's mother would accept that her children had lives and interests apart from her. She would not expect constant and/or daily contact and would not rely upon her children exclusively for her transport, or to provide her with services available from other sources. In John's case, if he had been raised in a nonenmeshed family, he would have been encouraged to pursue educational interests and a career that interested him, instead of having to satisfy his parents' dream.

As you read these two vignettes, did you see some similarities between Barbara and John's situations and your own experiences with one or more members of your family? If so, you may be sacrificing important parts of your life to take care of others because of your emotional susceptibility. That is, if you are very open to "catching" other people's feelings, you may have been conditioned to assume responsibility for those feelings.

Are You Enmeshed?

How can you tell if you are suffering the effects of family enmeshment, emotional susceptibility, and whether you are overresponsible? You can get a good indication of the extent of your enmeshment, emotional susceptibility, and sense of overresponsibility by answering the following questions:

- Do you have one or more family members to whom you cannot refuse any requests, no matter how much you must personally sacrifice to fill the request?

- Do you feel responsible for the happiness and well-being of any or all adult members of your family?

- Do you work hard to ensure that harmony reigns among the adults in your family?

- Do you end up assuming most or all of the responsibility for how well family events function?

- Were you allowed to make personal decisions that were supported by your parent(s) when you were a child or a teenager?

- Are you blamed when things go wrong or events do not flow smoothly in your family?

- Do you feel as if some family members take advantage of your good nature?

- Do you often find that you are doing things you do not want to do because a family member made you feel guilty?

- Does it greatly upset you to say no to a family member?

- How have you fulfilled one or both parents' dream, e.g., taking music or ballet lessons, playing sports, or engaging in any other activity that you did not wish to do?

- If one of your parents frowns, do you immediately assume you did something to upset him/her?

- Do you often feel you are overwhelmed with family responsibilities and yearn to take better care of yourself?

- Have you, or do you, make numerous personal sacrifices for your family's benefit? Do those family members for whom you sacrificed seem unappreciative?

If you are experiencing the effects of family enmeshment, the long-term negative effects can manifest as any or all of the following:

- physical health problems, such as high blood pressure

- emotional health problems, such as depression

- spiritual health problems, such as feeling that life is meaningless

- relational problems, such as the inability to form lasting relationships

- the feeling that life is passing you by

- the feeling of being closed in, trapped or stuck without meaningful connections

- the desire to get away from parents or other relatives most times when you have to interact with them

- a sense of powerlessness to effect changes in oneself

- lack of control (helplessness to effect changes in others when their behavior has a negative impact on you)

Personal Descriptors

We will begin this journey of self-exploration by examining the extent to which you become enmeshed and/or overwhelmed by others' emotions. If most of the following descriptors fit you, then you may be at risk of being enmeshed, overwhelmed, or damaged psychologically and/or emotionally. You may be trying to cope simultaneously with your emotions, and with those of others, without realizing when this is happening. You may tend to become aware of what took place only in hindsight.

Furthermore, regardless of your resolve not to let this take place, it continues to happen over and over again, usually to your detriment. You may even find yourself engaging in self-destructive behaviors or in behaviors that cause you to feel shame and/or guilt. You may have tried to guard against becoming overly involved with others' needs but, so far, you have not managed to change your behavior. Do many of the following descriptions apply to you?

- Do you get depressed when others are depressed?

- Do you think you have too much empathy?

- Do you seem to stay more emotionally intense than others around you?

- Do you often feel that you are being manipulated by others?

- Do you have difficulty shutting off difficult feelings (e.g., guilt and shame)?

- Do you suspect that others take advantage of you because you care about them?

- Do you find yourself in situations you don't like or have not chosen because of someone's influence or persuasiveness?

- Do you want to please others and/or maintain harmony, no matter what it costs you?

- Do you try hard not to say or do anything that might upset another person?

- Do you suppress your feelings frequently to take care of someone else who seems to need comfort?

If you found that several of these descriptions fit you, and you are troubled by the feelings or attitudes, then you may very well tend to become enmeshed and/or overwhelmed by others' emotions. You may perceive yourself as soft-hearted, caring too much, or being overly empathic, but it is much more likely that you fail to, or are unable to effectively shield yourself from catching others' emotions.

Catching Emotions

There is considerable evidence that emotions can be "caught." For example, in the book, *Emotional Contagion* (1994), Elaine Hatfield and others present research on catching emotions, emotional susceptibility, and emotional infectors. In addition, there is a body of psychotherapeutic literature that describes concepts about getting rid of unwanted feelings by projecting them onto another person (Brown 1998). This process can be made even more complicated when the projector stays in touch with those projected feelings and manipulates them so that the other person then acts on the projected and incorporated feeling. This is called *projective identification*.

There are additional research studies on who catches these feelings, why, how the catcher identifies and acts on them, and what keeps some people immune to the entire process, such as those people described in *Emotional Contagion* by Hatfield and colleagues (1994). The concept of projective identification is a major premise that will be explored in this book. Other topics included that are intended to help you:

- Identify attitudes and behaviors that will provide clues about the extent to which you "catch" the emotions of others

- Understand how your emotions are triggered and manipulated by *internal* forces

- Understand how your emotions are triggered and manipulated by *external* forces

- Understand the importance of psychological boundaries and family-of-origin issues

- Guide you in developing "emotional shielding"

- Provide you with suggestions, exercises, and activities to promote your personal growth

The Positive Aspects of Caring

Although considerable distress can result from feeling that you care too much, or that you have too much empathy, there are some positive aspects that must also be taken into account. The basic traits of caring for others and feeling empathy are certainly not undesirable. They are essential for developing and maintaining long-lasting and satisfying relationships. Creating such relationships is a desirable and praiseworthy goal that helps to give meaning and purpose to our lives. We want and need these types of relationships.

Relationships can flourish when there is *mutual*

- respect

- positive regard (admiration)

- caring and nurturance

- desire for each other's well-being

- interdependence

- attention to basic relationship needs

- joy in the relationship

- appreciation and acceptance

The key word is *mutual*; nevertheless, it is important for this discussion that the focus remains on you. The behaviors and attitudes listed for relationships to flourish are intended to show you that the very traits needed for satisfying relationships are embedded in the same traits that are causing you distress, i.e., your ability to catch others' emotions.

On the one hand, you probably have some helpful characteristics for developing and maintaining satisfying relationships, but they may be also contributing to your distress. Characteristics such as these are helpful to relationships:

- being open

- trusting

- valuing harmony

- wanting to be loved and to love in return

- willingness to care for others

However, these same characteristics can affect how you respond to others in ways that are not in your best interest, and may even be self-destructive. These positive traits will be discussed in greater detail in chapter 5.

Useful Definitions

At this point, it may be helpful to provide some brief definitions and/or to describe some terms that may be unfamiliar to you, which are used throughout the book. These terms are a major part of the discussion: empathy, emotional susceptibility, emotional shielding, external forces, internal forces, and the psychological terms, projection, splitting, identification, and projective identification. Definitions for these terms follow.

Empathy

In recent years, this term has become widely used as synonymous with sympathy. However, *empathy and sympathy are not the same.* As used here, *empathy* is defined as entering the inner world of the other person and feeling what he/she is feeling at that moment, without losing the sense of your own self. This definition holds empathy to be a temporary "emotional merger," one where you do not become totally as one with the other person because you hold on to your perception of yourself as a different person—a separate individual.

In other words, when you are empathic, you do not become enmeshed or overwhelmed with the other person. Becoming lost, enmeshed, overwhelmed, or otherwise staying merged with the person is *not* empathy. There may be many reasons why you become lost, etc., but that state is not empathy: you do not maintain a separate and distinct sense of yourself as an individual, as being apart from the other person.

This sense, or perception of yourself, as separate is called the "observing ego" in the psychological literature. It is expected to emerge around the ages of twelve to thirteen in the course of normal psychological development (Kernberg 1990). Some people have inadequately developed their observing egos, and this can contribute to getting lost, etc., in others' feelings.

Sympathy and empathy are different states, although there may be some relatedness. *Empathy* was defined earlier as *feeling what the other person is feeling. Sympathy* is defined as *thinking about what the other person may be feeling but not experiencing the same feelings yourself.* There is some distance, or detachment, with sympathy that is lacking with empathy. You may use the same or similar words when responding sympathetically and empathetically, but with sympathy, the only feelings involved are yours and what you may think or imagine the other person's are. You do not feel what the other person feels.

Emotional Susceptibility

As noted before, there is considerable evidence that the phenomenon of "emotional contagion" exists, which leads to this point: if emotions can be caught, then there are people who can "catch" them (Hatfield, Cacioppo, and Rapson 1994). Clearly, some people are better at catching emotions than others. Your *emotional susceptibility* is determined by the extent to which you "catch" others' emotions.

Illustrations of emotional contagion abound. Actors are adept at portraying characters who can cause you to laugh, cry, become afraid, and feel the entire spectrum of human emotions. You "catch" the portrayed emotion. Many parents are able to sense what their children feel. Emotional contagion takes place when you interact with a depressed or grieving person, and you become sad or "down." Good feelings also can be caught. For example, it's hard not to smile or feel good in the presence of someone who is openly happy. In that case, you are "catching" the emotion of happiness or pleasure.

Emotional Shielding

You also can shield yourself from catching another's emotions, and from having your emotions triggered. Emotional shielding is an outcome of strong psychological boundaries that protect you when you encounter external forces that seem threatening to such boundaries. A strong developed self protects you from internal forces that seem threatening. Emotional shielding is employed to protect the self from experiencing an assault by either the emotions of others or from personal emotions, such as guilt and shame. This shielding allows the self to remain at some distance from emotional onslaughts that have the potential for allowing the self to be manipulated, overwhelmed, put in danger of being destroyed, fused, or to lose control. The self perceives a potential danger to its well-being and the protective devices of shielding come into play to keep it safe. Of course, all of this happens on an unconscious level without conscious volition.

A key component in emotional shielding is the strength of your psychological boundaries against external forces. Weak, inefficient, and/or lack of psychological boundaries lead to emotional susceptibility, and that can lead to your "catching" the emotions of others. The more emotional susceptibility you have, the more likely you are to "catch" others' emotions. That state can leave you open to being manipulated or overwhelmed, and so forth. The ideal is to have sufficiently strong boundaries to prevent your "catching" another's emotions, but still allow you to be empathic.

Your internal defense system is also important because you want to have access to your emotions and not be overly defended. When you are too defended, a large part of your self is unavailable because it is too dangerous for your self to realize the existence of some of its parts. So, you defend it with a strong defense system, e.g., denial and repression. This, too, takes place on an unconscious level. Emotional shielding against internal forces also must be strong, but it must also be capable of being lowered, to permit appropriate access to important material in the unconscious.

External Forces

Simply put, external forces are the wishes, desires, projections, and manipulations of other people who have you as their target. These people want something from you and consider you available to meet their needs, whether or not you are willing or cooperative. They use you to meet their personal goals and needs, without any regard for you as a separate and unique individual. You are exploited for the other person's personal gain.

For example, in the story that opens this chapter, Barbara's mother wants Barbara to be responsible for her emotional well-being. Instead of taking steps to reduce her loneliness by reaching out to others, Barbara's mother became more dependent. The early parent-child connection between Barbara and her mother ensured that Barbara would feel enough guilt and shame that she would assume the unnecessary responsibility for her mother's well-being. This, of course, was at some emotional and psychological costs for Barbara.

On the other hand, John seems to have reached his limit for pleasing his parents. They wanted him to get a law degree and he gave them their wish. However, he also decided that "enough was enough," and that he wanted to live his own life and follow his own dream for a career, not his parents'.

If you have insufficient boundary strength and emotional shielding, these external forces demand, or force, you to incorporate them into your own thinking; and then to act in such a way as to give exploiters what they want. Your openness and concern, although admirable traits in other situations, in this instance, are used against your best interests.

Internal Forces

There are also internal forces that cooperate with external forces, such as your:

- underdeveloped narcissism (see the section "Adult Self-Focus" below for a discussion of healthy adult narcissism)

- old parental messages

- need to be loved

- desire for power and control

- strength of self-confidence and self-esteem

- understanding of your personal desires and needs

The result of such cooperation may be that your emotions will be triggered, which may lead to undesirable and distressing feelings and acts. Much of the text of this book deals with learning about your internal forces, determining how best to guard against their impact, and how to grow stronger, more usable boundaries that will protect you, without shutting off access to your own emotions.

The definitions of splitting, projection, identification, and projective identification are taken from the literature of psychotherapy (Klein 1952; Mahler, Pine, and Bergman 1975; Kernberg 1990) and are closely intertwined with the internal forces. The important points to remember while you read and absorb the definitions are these:

- everyone does employ these processes

- they are not "wrong"

- they are unconscious or nonconscious processes

- our early experiences play a major role in their internal formation.

Splitting

Splitting is a way the self gets rid of something that is unwanted or undesirable. Whatever is unwanted or undesirable that cannot be accepted or tolerated is split off, so that the self can maintain its integrity, i.e., it does not have (or own) the something that is so threatening.

For example, suppose that your self does not want to accept that you really do feel rage for a parent. Part of your self's integrity is the belief that your parent is wonderful and you are pleased and grateful to have such a parent. So, to get rid of the distressing feeling, you split off your anger/rage, and then your self can remain unaware of the rage or anger, which is precisely what your self wants.

The split-off anger is handled in one of two ways, projection or repression. Projection is described in the next section. *Repression* of the split-off anger allows you to push it into your unconscious mind and wall it off, so that it cannot get to your conscious mind. If you are not aware of it, then it does not exist for you. That does not mean that it doesn't have any impact or influence; it does. However, its impact and influence are indirect, and it will be difficult or impossible to see the connection between the split-off repressed anger, and how its influence is manifested. For example, there can be the following consequences:

- physical consequences, such as hypertension and heart problems

- relationship consequences, such as the inability to form meaningful relationships

- effects on psychological growth and development, such as the inability to appropriately be assertive

- failure to develop in unexpected ways, such as the inability to overcome an excessive need for attention and admiration

- an impact on one's self-perception, such as low self-esteem

- inappropriate displacement, such as irritation or anger at your child or spouse for inconsequential things, when you are really angry at yourself

Projection

It is possible that some, or even many, of our reactions, hunches, and feelings about other people are projections. As stated above, projections occur when we split off a piece of self, and place it on or in another person, and then react to that person as if he or she were the split-off piece. Generally, the reality is that the other person is not entirely as you perceive him/her. However, you continue to react to that person in this way.

Let's go back to a situation where you feel unwanted anger for a parent, and you do not want to accept the truth that you have split off your anger and repressed it. If you were to *project* your anger, however, instead of repressing it, you would project it onto another person, and then think that the person you projected your anger to was angry; so, you would react to the perceived anger. The other person might or might not be angry. However, your reaction would be out of sync with what that person is really feeling, and this could lead to misunderstandings and misinterpretations.

Think of the times when you kept silent because you assumed you knew what the other person wanted, was feeling, or would appreciate. For example, the following story illustrates how personal needs can be projected. Rebecca's sister was preparing to go out on a date that was very important to her and she had taken pains with her makeup and dress. She came downstairs as soon as her date arrived, and it was only then that Rebecca noticed that her sister had on too much perfume and that her earrings did not match. She did not say anything because she thought it would embarrass her sister in front of her date. When her sister returned home, she jumped all over Rebecca because she felt that Rebecca had let her down.

These are examples of possible projections. You may have had a particular need or feeling, but you projected that need or feeling onto the other person, and your response to that person, e.g., keeping silent, was made on the basis of what *you* would have wanted. You gave the other person what you consciously thought he/she wanted, but, in reality, you were meeting your own unconscious needs. Projecting can become a part of your emotional susceptibility, and you will want to become more aware of how it works, so that when you might engage in projecting, you will be able to recognize what you are doing.

Identification

Identification is a psychological process that begins in infancy whereby we become socialized, incorporate values, and begin to form beliefs and attitudes. This is not a conscious undertaking; it is a part of who we become. The bond between mother and child facilitates early identification when the child is open to mother's unconscious needs, beliefs, and so forth. The child incorporates these, and they become reinforced by other people in the child's environment. Humans identify by incorporating and making those incorporations into parts of themselves. This process continues throughout one's lifetime. Thus, identification is ever-present.

These identifications are not fixed. They can be modified with considerable conscious effort. First, you have to understand what they are, and that is very difficult, but it can be done. Another piece of information suggested in this book is that you learn to be more aware of those occasions when you are engaged in identifying. You can learn to ask yourself: "With what am I identifying? And what are my possible reasons for such identification?"

Projective Identification

The processes of splitting, projecting, and identifying can combine to produce *projective identification*. This is an abstract and complex phenomenon that can take some time to understand and accept. After all, we are unable to observe it objectively, and must rely upon our internal experience for validation. Nevertheless, projective identification is a major aspect of emotional shielding.

Projective identification involves a sender of emotions and a receiver. What happens is that:

1. A split-off piece of the sender's self is projected onto another person, that is, the receiver.

2. Then, the receiver incorporates and identifies with all, or some, of the split-off piece, making the split-off piece a part of him/herself.

3. The sender, however, does not push the split-off piece onto the receiver just to get rid of it. Oh no. He/she stays in touch with that aspect of self that was split off.

4. The receiver has made part or all of the split-off piece a part of him/herself, but the split-off piece is not entirely free from the sender. It is still connected to the sender.

5. Now, the sender can manipulate the split-off but still connected piece, which then causes the receiver to act on the connected piece.

Let's go back to the example about you feeling anger at your parent again. With projection, the sender (you) gets rid of your anger by pushing it on someone else. Suppose that that person was not angry and did *not* accept the projected anger, although you were reacting to him/her as if he or she was angry. Then, that person would not be open to manipulation.

With projective identification, however, the receiver would identify with all or part of the projected anger and be manipulated by your connection to the anger and become angry when he or she had not been previously angry. Have you ever had something similar happen to you?

You found yourself in a situation where you became angry or enraged, and some part of you wondered where all your anger was coming from? Yes, you knew that you had some reason to be annoyed, but why so much anger? Furthermore, you found yourself saying and/or doing uncharacteristic things as a result of your anger. Were you puzzled or appalled at yourself? The previous example of an angry parent-child interaction illustrates how such a situation comes about.

Your anger might have been the result of a projective identification. You may have "caught" the projected emotion, identified with part or all of it, and made it a part of your self. Then, the other person manipulated his/her split-off anger, that you had incorporated, and then you acted from that manipulated part.

Defending yourself against projections and projective identification is not an easy task, but it is possible to learn how to mount defenses. Although projective identification is both external and internal, and it takes place on unconscious levels, some headway can be made by understanding what your internal state contributes to the process. The next step is to figure out how that internal state can be strengthened to resist identifying with projections.

Personal Growth and Development

Personal growth does not focus exclusively on psychological growth. It is also concerned with many other parts of your life and self, including the following aspects of your character and personality:

- emotional development

- relationships

- creativity

- spirituality

The state of your physical being is, of course, basic. For, without your body, there is no "you" to have a "self." Your physical being has an impact on all other aspects of your being, and the presence or absence of disease (whether chronic and/or acute), nutrition, exercise, proper amount of rest, and so forth, significantly influence other parts of your being and your life.

Psychological Growth

Early relationships and experiences play major roles in our psychological development, and they continue to exert influences throughout our lives. The mother-infant/child relationship sets a tone and pattern for our:

- self-perception
- self-esteem
- self-confidence
- self-efficacy
- values
- attitudes
- beliefs
- relationships
- interactions with the world

Note that the term "mother" is used here to mean a child's major caretaker, as that person may not be the child's mother. Psychological literature refers to "mother" and states that the mother-child relationship is like no other; but present-day reality is such that the mother may not be the person most intimately involved with the infant and taking care of its moment-to-moment needs. While you read, adjust your thinking to whatever fits your situation.

A major task of psychological growth and development is to become a separate and distinct individual. To be fully grown means to gain a sense of who you are, as uniquely different from others, especially from your parents. The early parent-child bond tends to work against complete separation and the development of a self-identity that is yours and consciously chosen (*individuation*) because so many patterns of psychological interrelatedness can endure in maturity, i.e., the continuing impact of old parental messages.

The family of origin also plays a major role in development. Family characteristics, such as sibling relationships; extended family availability; employment; the presence or absence of physical, sexual and/or emotional abuse; and chronic or acute physical and/or mental illnesses all contribute to psychological growth and development.

Emotional Development

Emotional development is hard to separate from psychological development, but in this book, it is discussed as a separate topic to emphasize its importance in emotional susceptibility and emotional shielding. The first step in understanding the level of your emotional development is to become aware of what you are feeling. The "why" or other analyses can wait.

Your awareness of what you are feeling is critical for reducing emotional susceptibility. Too often, the feeling aroused by "catching" the other person's feeling is incorporated, but is not identified as such. Once you become involved or lost in that "caught" feeling you are not capable of separating what is *your* feeling from what belongs to the other person. You allow yourself to be taken over by the other person's feeling, which you now consider to be your feeling. You may term it empathy, but since there is no observing ego, i.e., the part of you that remains detached and connected to reality, the feelings become enmeshment, engulfment, or being overwhelmed instead of being empathic.

Your progress in emotional development was closely intertwined with your family-of-origin experiences. How emotions were expressed or not expressed, which emotions could be verbalized and which were to remain unspoken, how emotional expressions were received, and how valued your emotions were by the members of your family of origin all played important roles in your current level of emotional development.

You learned from birth on which emotional expressions were considered appropriate, and you have unconsciously continued to act on those lessons ever since. Learning about the following aspects of your emotional life can do much to help you develop better boundaries:

- the course of your emotional development

- your current emotional expressiveness

- your usual defenses, e.g., suppression

- your awareness of your need for improvement

You can also get a better sense of what you are feeling at any time which, in turn, can lead you to become more aware of when you may be experiencing projective identification. You may also gain a greater ability to withstand others' projections and learn to feel that these projections are not your responsibility.

Relationships

Relationships make us feel connected and reduce feelings of isolation and alienation. Indeed, many self-defeating behaviors are the end results of people trying to feel less lonely and alienated. The richness that meaningful and satisfying relationships bring to our lives cannot be overstated. Relationships have the power to make us feel these positive emotions:

- valued

- loved

- purposeful

- the sense of belonging

- life has meaning

- connected

Relationships also can be destructive and unrewarding. These are the relationships that you will want to evaluate, work to improve, or discard. It is important that you carefully examine all of your current relationships to determine whether you are being exploited, manipulated, and/or are the repository for another person's dissatisfactions. Also, you will need to determine what are the gaps in your current relationships. For example, do you have many current relationships or are they limited to a very few.

Examining your past relationships provides another source of valuable information. This examination can reveal if there is a pattern in your usual relationships. If there is a pattern, you can identify what was satisfying and rewarding, what you contributed to those relationships, when they stopped meeting your needs and, thus, were discarded. You can identify both positive and negative elements, which will assist you in reviewing your current relationship more objectively.

This review should include those relationships where you feel the most susceptible to catching the other person's emotions. These relationships have components intertwined with your psychological and emotional development that are not useful for you. Understanding what these components are will assist you in developing strategies to identify similar components in future relationships.

That understanding also will help you to build internal defenses that can keep you from automatically tuning in to manipulative persons, and will strengthen your psychological boundaries in ways that will not prevent the more positive aspects of your self from being lost or underused.

Adult Self-Focus

It is possible to have a healthy and appropriate *self-focus* (also called *healthy adult narcissism*) that protects the integrity of the self from emotional susceptibility where you are open to manipulation and exploitation by others. Healthy adult narcissism means that you have built and fortified your "self" and achieved the following:

- A viable self-identity that is yours, not what someone else wants you to be.

- Independence as an adult who also recognizes the need for interdependence.

- Management of your attention and admiration needs.
- A wide range of emotional expression that you can appropriately express.
- The ability to delay gratification to take care of others, when such care is needed.
- The understanding and acceptance of personal limitations.
- The love and acceptance of self.
- An appropriate sense of humor.
- The knowledge to use empathy without getting lost in others' feelings.
- The ability to be creative.

Creativity

Creativity is a major component of a healthy person's self-development and self-focus. As part of a plan to achieve greater personal growth, creativity becomes a necessary focus. Creativity is not limited to what is known as the fine and performing arts, i.e., music, art, dance, and drama. Being open to wonder, developing new ways of doing ordinary things, and constructing new and original concepts and things are all important aspects of creativity. This description allows for you to be creative in every part of your life, and does not depend on outside recognition. Changing your perception of creativity is a necessary first step. Recognizing opportunities for creative expression is another step. Here are some examples of creative expression in everyday life:

- A teacher develops a new method for helping a particular student learn.
- A workman jury-rigs a needed part for a building project.
- A father makes up a story to entertain his children.
- A parent creates a motivational reinforcement to get her teen to do chores, and it works.
- A mother puts ingredients together in a completely new way and produces a gourmet dish for the family dinner.
- A young woman has few clothes but she combines them so creatively that she always looks well dressed and attractive.

Creativity involves the ability to wonder. To wonder is to be open to "seeing" the beauty and originality in everyday life. It is an appreciation for the unexpected event that brings pleasure. It is taking the time to allow yourself and the world around you to be known and experienced. Opening yourself to wonder increases your ability to be creative. You become more perceptive, flexible, and willing to explore new ways of doing everything. Wonder expands your imagination.

Creativity is enhanced by these qualities:

- wonder

- imagination

- experience

- expression

The Spiritual Dimension

Many people equate the concept of spiritual activity with religion, but that is not how it is used in this book. Religion, faith, and belief are some of the ways in which the spiritual can be experienced and expressed, but they are not the only ways. This book uses the wider usage of the term to describe that which gives meaning and purpose to life, and can be found between the "Being" and the "Doing." Thus, the spiritual is unique to the individual and can be found and expressed in many ways including the following:

- uplifting rituals and practices

- positive ways of connecting to the universe and to others

- positive ways to reduce feelings of isolation and alienation

- positive ways to revive, refresh, and bring joy

Your personal growth will include a review of the spiritual side of your life, and a guide to a better understanding of how to tap the strength and power of your spirituality, as well as developing strategies for increasing it. This will give you a considerable resource that will help in building and strengthening your self, so that your emotional shielding will protect you, but also will allow the positive aspects of your self to be used properly. Your spiritual nature is important for the following reasons:

- It is a guide to self-affirming behavior.

- It allows you to access your underused inner resources.

- It provides you with a feeling of connectedness.

- It can help you to become less self-absorbed and more self-reflective.

- It can help you to develop personal meaning and greater purpose in your life.

● It can broaden your perspective of self, others, and the universe.

● It can provide support for those times when you fail to meet self-expectations.

There are discussions, exercises, and suggested activities throughout the book designed to provide you with a means to better understand and develop your spiritual resources.

Chapter 2

Emotional Susceptibility and Seduction

Rob was helping his wife Judy get everything ready for the holiday party for twenty people that they were hosting that evening. There were many last minute things to attend to, and the party had a special importance because both of their bosses were coming—with their wives. Rob and Judy both felt that their careers could be affected by the success or failure of their dinner party.

Rob had received a call from his father late that morning. His dad wanted Rob to come and get him to go out for a cup of coffee together. Rob had tried to explain about the dinner and all the work that was still to be done. His father had sounded very sad, telling Rob that he didn't want to interfere in his life, but there was no one else who cared about him. Rob felt torn, but he reacted to the sadness in his father's voice. He also felt guilty and ashamed of not being a better son to his lonely old father. Finally, Rob dropped what he was doing and took his father out to lunch, assuring the older man that it was not a problem, but then he felt guilty because he had abandoned his wife when she needed help. Needless to say, Rob did not feel good about anything that day.

Your Emotional Susceptibility

Before continuing with the text, it may be helpful to get some objective measure of your own susceptibility. The following questions describe some behaviors and attitudes that suggest a sensitivity to others' feelings, which may result in considerable personal cost to you, or in self-destructive behavior. Now, get a separate sheet of paper to write your answers to each question, and use the following scale to record your answers.

1—I never, or almost never do or feel this.

2—I seldom do or feel this.

3—I sometimes do or feel this.

4—I frequently do or feel this.

5—I almost always do or feel this.

Evidence of Emotional Susceptibility Scale

Using the scale listed above, answer how often you find yourself:

1. Doing something you do not want to do, just to please another person?

2. Wishing you had not let someone persuade you to do something that you felt was imprudent or wrong?

3. Wondering how you got into an uncomfortable situation?

4. Feeling like a fool for having trusted someone who betrayed you?

5. Giving of yourself to someone, only to find that he/she did not value you as you did him/her?

6. Surprised at the feeling, or intensity of feeling, you have in an interaction with another person?

7. Feeling beaten down by accusations that you act selfishly and that you are self-centered?

8. Becoming guilty or ashamed when someone tells you that you don't care for her/him, because if you did, you would do what he/she wants you to do?

9. Giving someone sympathy because he/she is sad, but then becoming and staying sad yourself?

10. Interacting with someone who is angry and frustrated, and when it's time to leave, you find yourself in an emotional tailspin, when you were okay before the interaction took place?

11. Working hard to ensure harmony and feeling guilty and responsible when there is conflict?

After you rate each item, review your ratings and place a checkmark (X) by the two or three most distressing behaviors or attitudes. These are the ones you will want to have as your top priority for making important changes.

Scoring Your Emotional Susceptibility

45 to 55: You exhibit considerable emotional susceptibility.

35 to 44: You exhibit frequent emotional susceptibility that produces distress in your life.

25 to 34: You exhibit sufficient emotional susceptibility to be troubling to you.

24 and below: You may be emotionally susceptible from time to time, but not often.

At this point, the causes of your susceptibility will not be addressed. The focus is on establishing what you may be doing, thinking, and/or feeling that leads to your "catching" others' emotions, and the degree of distress your emotional susceptibility causes you.

Considerable Susceptibility (45 to 55)

If your scores fall in this range, you are probably experiencing frequent distress due to your inability to resist catching others' emotions, and/or feeling that you must please them. There are times when you find yourself acting in a way that is inconsistent with your intentions, values, morals, or self-interest. The residual feelings stay with you for a long time, and you may berate yourself, feel guilty or ashamed, and make vows to change only to find yourself again in the same or a similar situation a short time later.

Frequent Susceptibility (35 to 44)

You tend to find yourself in situations where your emotions are triggered by others. You may even realize what is happening at the time, but you feel helpless to stop it, or to prevent it from happening again. You may even chide yourself and make plans for how to prevent it in the future, and on occasion, you are able to control your emotional susceptibility. However, all too often, it still happens, and you are distressed at your inability to adequately shield yourself from others' emotions.

Troubling Susceptibility (25 to 34)

You may experience catching others' emotions infrequently. You probably have the needed elements in your character to shield yourself emotionally, but are unable to employ them in certain situations. Your susceptibility is limited and focused.

Below 24 on the Scale

If you scored 24 or below on the scale, you probably have few or no problems with emotional susceptibility, and are not reading this book. If you are reading the book, you will want to review your ratings and decide how honest you were when you rated your answers to the questions.

Faulty Assumptions

Some of your susceptibility stems from faulty assumptions you may have about what you should, or ought, to do and feel. Such assumptions are termed "faulty" because they are neither rational nor logical; they are unrealistic expectations that you have incorporated and internalized to your detriment. Faulty assumptions are never helpful, yet you continue to act on them, usually on an unconscious level.

Faulty assumptions arise, in part, from the spoken and unspoken values, attitudes, and expectations that your parents communicated to you from birth. Your desire to please your parent(s), the reinforcement you received, and the larger culture's expectations and reinforcement all combined to produce these faulty assumptions.

Scoring Your Faulty Assumptions

Rate each assumption in the Faulty Assumptions Scale below, using the following numerical values:

1—This does not fit me.

2—This belief or attitude seldom influences my behavior or attitudes.

3—This belief or attitude does influence my behavior and attitudes on occasion.

4—This is a belief or attitude of mine that influences many of my behaviors and attitudes.

5—This is a core belief of mine, and I do believe it is true.

Common Faulty Assumptions

1. I am responsible for how others feel.

2. If there is disharmony, it's my fault, even if I am not involved.

3. I must never do or say anything that could upset another person.

4. If I engage in any conflict, that means I will be abandoned or destroyed.

5. When someone makes me feel good, that means he/she likes me.

6. When someone likes me that means they will take care of me, and that person has my best interests at heart.

7. I feel I need to do things I do not want to do, so others will be happy and approve of me.

8. It's selfish to put my needs before others' needs.

9. If I am agreeable, people will like me.

10. If I always say pleasant things, people will like me.

11. If I take care of them, people will like me.

12. If I love someone enough, he/she will love me in return.

13. I can feel worthwhile only if I have someone to love me.

14. I can feel alive and excited only when I'm with the person I love.

Scoring Your Faulty Assumptions

60 to 70: You are considerably influenced by faulty assumptions.

50 to 59: You are very influenced by faulty assumptions.

40 to 49: You are somewhat influenced by faulty assumptions.

30 to 39: You are seldom influenced by faulty assumptions.

Below 30: You may have some faulty assumptions, but you are not often influenced by them.

Other People's Feelings

You are not responsible for the feelings that others experience. You cannot cause others to have a particular feeling: they either choose to have the feeling, or they identified with all or part of a projection, and are now acting on it. Either way, their feelings are their responsibility, not yours.

However, you may have incorporated the faulty assumption that you are responsible for other people's feelings early in your life through one or both parents' expectations that you were to be responsible for his/her emotional well-being. Or, you may be acting on a learned assumption that holds you responsible for how others feel.

No matter what your reason for holding this belief might be, it is a *faulty* assumption and it contributes to your emotional susceptibility. For example, a parent may manipulate you in the following ways by:

- Asking you, "Don't you want to make me feel good"?

- Telling you that you caused him or her to feel a particular feeling

- Criticizing you for not paying enough attention to their feelings

- Expecting you to take care of him or her, and saying so on numerous occasions

It is not easy to overcome this particular faulty assumption, especially if it has been ingrained from childhood experiences. Indeed, you may be acting without conscious thought. Nevertheless, examining your behavior consciously is the first step in changing it.

Harmony and Disharmony

There is another faulty assumption closely allied with the faulty assumption that you are responsible for other people's well-being. That is the assumption where you believe that you are the one who must ensure that there is always harmony, and, if disharmony exists, you must deal with it, make it go away, and restore harmony to the situation. This faulty assumption can keep you on edge and anxious looking for hints of disharmony, so that you can spring into action.

Although harmony is desirable, always having to maintain harmony works against your best interests and your well-being. You can be manipulated by others who will use your desire for harmony and your good nature to get you to do what they want you to do: you may go along with whatever it is they want just to be agreeable, or to keep the peace.

For example, you may have an aunt who wants you to run errands for her, even though she can easily do them herself. The fact that you are inconvenienced is of no concern to her. But you don't want to say "no" to her because that would upset her, and you feel that you must preserve harmony at all costs. The intensity of the need you have for harmony, and the assumption that you are responsible for maintaining it, can leave you at the mercy of other people's wishes and needs.

Another issue to consider is that you may tend to avoid even the slightest hint of conflict, either personal or the conflicts of others. This can lead you to the perception that conflict in itself is always destructive. This, in turn, can lead you to fear that either you and/or the other person will be destroyed if you engage in any kind of conflict. So, you may act to prevent conflict, or you will be agreeable to ensure that conflict does not emerge. What you probably need to learn is that it is possible for conflict to be constructive and to strengthen relationships.

No one person is responsible for maintaining harmony. Everyone bears some responsibility for situations to be harmonious, and it is a bit grandiose to expect that you are sufficiently powerful to ensure that harmony will always prevail. Just think for a moment about how you feel when, in spite of your best efforts, you cannot make a conflicted situation harmonious.

For example, suppose there was a quarrel between your brother and a distant cousin at your last family holiday dinner. In such a situation, you might have felt a sense of failure. You might have felt that you were somehow flawed because, if you were not flawed, you would have been able to stop the quarrel, and the meal would have been more harmonious for everyone. At the end of the dinner, you might have thought, "Next time I will try even harder." In addition to being a faulty assumption, such thinking is counterproductive to your own well-being.

Upsetting Others

How do you feel when someone gets upset about something you said? Do you rush to explain, change what you meant, or try to soothe that person? Do you tend to be tentative and careful in what you say to others for fear of upsetting them, and then rationalize your carefulness with the thought that you are just being sensitive? If you answer any, or all, of these questions with "yes," then you have made a faulty assumption.

When others get upset at something you said, you may experience all or some of the following thoughts:

- They won't like me.
- They think I'm insensitive.
- I feel guilty because I did something wrong.
- I should not have said what I did because it made him/her upset.
- It upsets me when I say or do something that causes someone to be upset.
- How could I do something so stupid?

All these thoughts are focused on you and your feelings. In one sense, you are taking responsibility for your feelings; but in some respects, not entirely. You do not allow the other person to take responsibility for his/her feelings, and neither do you accept that you did not *cause* the other person to have that particular feeling.

If, or when, something you say triggers another person's feelings, that's all it is—a trigger. Their feelings are triggered because of *their* issues, unfinished business, current emotional state, and so forth. The other person could choose not to become upset, or to work on her/his underlying issues so that their feelings are not triggered, or choose to do other personal growth and development work. However, those are personal issues for that person; you have nothing to do with this work. *Your job is to work on your own issues and concerns.*

Having to stay alert all the time to ensure that you are not on the verge of saying something that might upset someone else is emotionally draining; and can translate into physical tension. It is also futile because there is always someone to get upset about something. Taking that stance also means that you must be alert to any nonverbal cues of distress that others display, and, as you will see later, that can open you up to being emotionally manipulated.

Conflict

Ed cringed as his sister ran into the room shouting that she couldn't stand their mother one more minute. His sister and their mother were constantly at odds over the least little thing, and both looked to him to take sides or resolve the conflict. But he felt caught in the middle. He was often torn because he could see both of their points of view, but when he tried to make peace, his mother and his sister both accused him of favoring the other. He really wanted to get out of the middle of their conflicts, but he was afraid that if he withdrew, then he would lose their love and affection.

Conflicts can range in intensity from mild disagreements about something of little or no consequence to fierce battles. The most common perception about conflict deems it bad, undesirable, attacking, and destructive. If this is your definition of conflict, then you probably do everything in your power to avoid it. You may even give in, do what someone else wants you to do, or act against your values and principles in order to avoid engaging in conflict.

Conflict is unavoidable. If you choose to avoid a conflict with another person, you may end up with internal conflict. Furthermore, your avoidance may be misinterpreted by the other person, leading him or her to believe that you can be manipulated to do whatever that person wants, and he/she will be correct in that assessment. Your faulty assumption about conflict can put you in this position.

Conflict can be constructive and help to strengthen relationships. Disagreements can be a way to clarify values and opinions, reveal beliefs and attitudes, and understand what is significant and important for each other. Conflicts do not have to be win-lose situations; each person can win. You do not have to give in to the other person, nor they to you. When you are so afraid of losing the relationship if you were to disagree with the other person, you do not have a strong relationship; moreover you may be opening yourself up to being manipulated by him/her.

What could be helpful for you are two strategies: to become more comfortable with conflict, and to learn new ways of behaving in conflict situations. Both of these strategies are discussed addressed in chapters 7 through 10 dealing with personal growth.

Abandoned or Destroyed

The two basic fears we all have to differing degrees are these: the fear of being abandoned, and the fear of being destroyed. These fears appear to be present from birth, remain on the unconscious level, and can be components in the relationships we form. That is, we are attracted to others with the expectations that they will neither abandon nor destroy us.

These fears can be triggered easily when you have not fortified your "self" to have confidence that you can survive independently from another person. When you have a fortified self, you understand what loneliness is, and you can make constructive use of it rather than becoming anxious and forming unproductive and unsatisfying relationships to avoid feeling lonely.

Your openness to catching another's emotions can cause your fears to become triggered, or lead you to incorporate and act on the other person's projective identifications, thereby intensifying your fears of being abandoned or destroyed, and, at the same time, acting on the sender's fears. Working on your personal growth and development can help to fortify your "self" so that these fears are not easily triggered.

If the other person fears either abandonment or destruction, and you catch and identify with those fears, you will act to prevent those fears from becoming true, which is what the other person will have wanted or intended in the first place.

One of the topics addressed in chapter 6 presents suggestions for understanding how you may have acted on your fears of being abandoned or destroyed throughout your relationships; how these fears may be triggered for you, and short-term and long-term strategies that can help prevent these fears from being triggered. Also discussed are suggestions for what to do when they are triggered, and how to consciously recognize that these fears are being triggered.

Feeling Good and Being Liked

Olga was berating herself the morning after a party for having behaved as she had. She had drunk too much and now she had a hangover and was cringing at her memories of the party. Drinks she hadn't wanted had been urged on her and she had felt it would be impolite to refuse. Then, she had participated in an impromptu wet T-shirt contest. Later she found someone she felt attracted to, he kept flattering her and she wanted to keep his attention and interest. One thing had led to another and now she was disgusted with herself.

The desire to be liked is both healthy and appropriate. However, when wanting to be liked is a *basic* need, it is neither healthy nor appropriate, and can lead to doing things that are inconsistent with your morals, values, principles, and standards. Violations of these core attitudes and beliefs produce considerable guilt, shame, and other indications of psychological distress.

If you hold the faulty assumption that those who make you feel good do so because they like you, then you may experience the fear of abandonment or destruction that was described in the previous section. You may be willing to go along with what another person proposes simply because he/she makes you feel valued, important, and good. The underlying assumption that might lead you astray is that *the other person always has your best interest at heart.* That may or may not be the case.

Of course it is possible—even likely—that others do care for you and they do want you to feel good. You may have friends, lovers, and family members who meet this description, and when true, they can provide valuable emotional support and comfort. However, if you are finding that your emotional susceptibility is causing you distress, then you should consider the very real possibility that some of the people whom you think care for you make you feel good to meet *their* needs, and they may be manipulating you by means of your faulty assumption. Yes, they will like you so long as they can manipulate you to meet their needs, but that is not in your best interest.

You will want to examine your need to be liked, the extent to which you compromise your values, and so forth, to please another person so that he/she will continue to like you. You will also want to examine the psychological and emotional costs you pay for continuing to hold and act on this faulty assumption. There are exercises in chapters 7 through 10 to develop your self-reliance so that you can become less dependent on needing others to like you, without losing your healthy desire to be liked.

Your Best Interests and Others

The faulty assumption that others have your best interests at heart is similar in many respects to the faulty assumption that those who make you feel good do so because they like you, previously discussed. The major differences are these:

- the belief that liking equates with caring

- the unrealistic assumption that others have a responsibility to take care of you

- the belief that you need someone to take care of you

- the belief that the other person is not independent

You may hold this faulty assumption: When you like someone, you do what you can to take care of that person with the hope and expectation that your caring will be reciprocated. Over time, you may have been repeatedly disappointed. But your disappointments may not have deterred you, and you continue to give of yourself and receive little or no caring in return.

It is wonderful to be in a relationship with someone who does have your best interests at heart, someone you can trust not to hurt you, someone who does their best to take care of you. This is the basis for a deep, meaningful, satisfying relationship. It's both an ideal and realistic possibility. However, it is unlikely that you are reading this book because you have such a relationship, or have had many such relationships. It is much more likely that you have been disappointed many times and have experienced less than satisfying relationships.

Trust

Not trusting anyone to have your best interests at heart is not a desirable condition. You want to strike a reasonable balance between not trusting anyone and trusting everyone. Also, you will need to gain a clearer understanding of what constitutes reasonable limits on your expectations of others, even those who like you. Yes, you should be able to trust your family, friends, and other loved ones, but there are also limits as to what you should expect from them.

Then, too, there are those who are friendly and/or appear to be loving but, in reality, they use others to meet their personal needs. It is a mistake to expect such people to have your best interests at heart. What will be helpful is to be open to the best interpretation, e.g., others do like you and will care for you, but you must understand that their caring has limits. You must also be willing to wait for your awareness of the strength (or weakness) of the relationship to emerge. You can help yourself by being willing to take care of yourself, and to not make demands on others or place unrealistic expectations on them.

Wanting Others' Approval

Karen pushed the phone away from her ear because her husband was yelling at her. She had called him to let him know that he would have to fix dinner for the children as she had to babysit her sister's children. Her husband was upset because this was the second time this week that she sat with the children so her sister could go out, and she had promised him that she would not let her sister manipulate her into babysitting again, except in dire emergencies. Karen knew that she was being manipulated, but she felt that her sister needed her and that she had to respond to that need regardless of the cost to her own family. Her sister praised her for being so helpful and Karen really liked hearing that, even though she was aware that she was being manipulated. Her sister had been able to manipulate her throughout their growing-up years, and that pattern continued now.

"I need to do things I do not want to do, so others will like me." Wanting the approval of others can be one of the most self-destructive and dangerous faulty assumptions; it can lead to feeling considerable guilt and shame. The assumption that, if you do something you do not wish to do, you will win the approval of another is definitely an assumption you want to eliminate. It does not matter if the other person is a family member, friend, or lover. This faulty assumption works against your best interests because of the following reasons:

- It gives power and control over you to the other person.

- It violates your personal standards.

- It ignores your personal values, morals, and beliefs.

- It does not allow you to hear your inner voice, the voice of your intuitive wisdom.

- It promotes your compliance with being manipulated by others.

- It fosters an unwise belief that compromises your personal integrity.

- It encourages actions inconsistent with your best interests.

However, you still will want to consider carefully what others want you to do, and evaluate the validity of the claims on your time and attention. For example, if your parent wants you to visit a sick friend or relative, you may want to honor their request. What is important is this: *No matter what someone else wants you to do, your motivation should not be to make that person like you. If you do what is requested, do it because you want to do it, not to be liked.*

When a request is made of you, there is also the possibility that, you are experiencing projective identification (see chapter 1 for the definition of this term), and your deep-seated need to be liked may be triggered.

The situation described at the beginning of this chapter with Rob and his father also illustrates how your emotional susceptibility can permit you to be manipulated into putting others' needs first, even when it's not warranted. Rob's father was able to trigger guilt and shame, which then led to Rob's doing what his father wanted him to do, at considerable cost to Rob and to his marital relationship.

When you have the opportunity, you may want to reflect on why your need to be liked is so strong. You may want to analyze why being liked is so important to you that you are willing to compromise significant parts of yourself, e.g., your values, to satisfy this need. You may also want to think deeply about your current and past relationships and identify when and how often your need to be liked resulted in you being persuaded to act in a way that caused you distress, because the act was a violation of your values, morals, and/or standards.

Self-Care

There is a vast difference between taking care of yourself appropriately and self-absorption. The first is a healthy response and the second reflects selfishness and underdeveloped narcissism.

It is not selfish to put your needs ahead of satisfying another's needs or desires *some of the time*. However, giving your needs top priority all of the time reflects a constant self-absorption that can impair your relationships. Nonetheless, always giving others' needs priority over your own implies that you consider yourself less important than others, and this attitude can promote emotional susceptibility.

It is, however, difficult to define or describe the phrase "some of the time" in this context. One reason for the difficulty is that even when you may think that you are putting another's needs first, you may be acting from your deep-seated need to be liked; not because of the other person's need or manipulation of you. In any case, there are definitely times when it is in your best interest to put your own needs first, but these times depend on the circumstances, the others involved, your relationships with them, and many other variables.

What can be described is the effect of this faulty assumption and an affirmation that your needs are important. Always putting others' needs ahead of your own can lead to your manipulation by others. They learn how to trigger your guilt and shame by calling you selfish even when you are not being selfish.

If you hold the assumption that it is selfish to put your needs ahead of satisfying others' wishes, then you are not taking good care of yourself. You will want to learn how to balance self-interest and the appropriate nurturing of others. For example, my priorities shift and change, but I always put my children's needs first. Other than that, sometimes I attend to my needs, and sometimes others' needs take priority. It depends on who, what, when, and how.

Being Agreeable

It is true that some people will like you if you are agreeable, but it is also true that some people will consider your agreeableness as an invitation to take advantage of you. Others may consider it merely superficial, and still others will wonder why you do not assert yourself more often.

The faulty assumption is that *you must agreeable for others to like you*. The other side is, of course, that others will not like you if you are not agreeable. Embedded in these assumptions is a deep-seated need to be liked by everyone. To achieve such amiability, you conceal your disagreements with others, fail to make your preferences and wishes known, do not assert yourself, and leave yourself open to being manipulated.

You may receive pleasure if others praise you for being so agreeable. After all, we all get tired of disagreements, hassles, and other unpleasant and upsetting situations. It can be very agreeable to interact with someone who is amiable and congenial. Do not try to lose this quality. It is one you want to keep. The difficulty with it comes when you make the assumption that you must be this way to be liked. You do not.

It is possible to continue being liked if you voice a different perspective or another opinion. Your likability will not vanish if you want something different from what another person wants. Your pleasant nature will not go up in smoke if you say "no" when you do not want to do something, particularly something someone else wants you to do. Furthermore, you can be assertive in other ways. Although there are some people who will not like you when you disagree with their point of view, you will find that there are many who will like you more, plus they will respect you.

The people who want you to be agreeable and do and say what they want you to do and say (and who don't like you if you disagree) want you to meet *their* needs regardless of the cost to you. Such people tend to be manipulative and exploitive in their relationships and do not really care about you as a person. They are only focused on what they want, and, if they can capitalize on your deep-seated need to be liked, they can manipulate you to do what they want.

Reflect on your need to be liked. Everyone *wants* to be liked, but not everyone *needs* to be liked. If you have this need, you may want to work at understanding it better, and to become more aware of how it may have been detrimental to your relationships and best interests over the years. Once you become aware of the extent to which this need may have contributed to unsatisfying and/or destructive relationships, to violations of your standards, and/or to self-destructive behavior, you can begin to make changes. See chapters 5 and 6 for strategies for change and for guides to greater self-understanding.

Saying Pleasant Things

The assumption that people will like you if you always say pleasant things is both a valid and a faulty assumption. Yes, it is nice to hear pleasant remarks; they can be uplifting and inspirational, and yes, people will like you. On the other hand, if the situation does not call for pleasantness, your remarks may irritate, offend, insult, denigrate, and so forth. You will not necessarily be liked for trying to be pleasant when the situation does not warrant it. In such a case, you are meeting your need to be liked, not assessing the situation and making a more appropriate response.

The opportunity for others to manipulate you is embedded in your desire to be so amiable. The threat, spoken or not, is that if you do not say what they want, they won't like you, and will leave you. What you may be battling, in part, is the fear that you will be abandoned and left alone.

Combating this fear is not easy, and it is cold comfort to know that everyone has it. Being abandoned is very scary, and people react in different ways to avoid experiencing the isolation and loneliness that result from abandonment. However, if what you are doing to avoid being abandoned results in distress, you may want to examine your need to be so compliant and your underlying fear. You may be overreacting to the mere thought of loneliness, which leads you to act in ways contrary to your best interest.

Consider having the goal of saying pleasant things only when warranted, and that are truthful and sincere. This would mean that you also intend to stop doing the following:

- making insincere remarks

- making untruthful comments

- being inauthentic

- saying pleasant things solely because of your own needs

Acting on these goals can help you reduce the likelihood of being manipulated by others. Becoming more authentic will increase the likelihood of you being liked, even when what you say is not pleasant, because you can be trusted to be truthful, sincere, and genuine.

Taking Care of Others

The assumption here goes, "*If I take care of them, people will like me.*" If you hold this assumption, it could be helpful to make some changes to it. For example, you could change it to "Some people will like me if I take care of them, some of the time." When you cling to this faulty assumption, you may find that you are being intrusive, failing to empower others to take care of themselves, exceeding the limits of your responsibility, and being taken advantage of continually.

It is true that some people will like you for acting on this assumption; but others will see it as a weakness, an opportunity for exploitation, or a signal that you consider the other person incompetent or inadequate. Some may even think that you have very low self-esteem. At some point, even those nearest and dearest to you will push you away, telling you that you are not needed to take care of them. They can take care of themselves, thank you very much.

This faulty assumption might be embedded in your family-of-origin issues, when at an early age, you were made to feel responsible for the emotional well-being of one or both parents. You might have internalized this expectation, acted on it then, and might continue to act on it today.

This expectation may have grown to the point where you came to believe that others, too, had such expectations of you, and being accepted and approved of by others depended on satisfying this expectation. If this is indeed what took place, it will be very hard to change. That's because, if this faulty assumption was embedded in the psychological development of your self from a very early age, it is largely unconscious. It can, however, be changed.

What you do not want to happen is that you become indifferent to others' needs and cease all of your nurturing activities. That would not help you or the other people in your life. What could be helpful would be to change the assumption that others look to you for their well-being all of the time. Infants and small children would be the exceptions to this.

Even spouses and adolescents do not need you to be responsible for all of their emotional and physical well-being. You may be responsible for some, but they also have a responsibility to themselves. You can become more aware of the limits of your responsibility and engage in self-exploration to better understand what is contributing to your faulty assumption. Much of this book is dedicated to helping you explore this.

Loving and Being Loved in Return

"I can feel worthwhile only if I have someone to love me." You may have to dig deep to see if you cling to this faulty assumption. But if, over time, you have been disappointed again and again by people whom you loved but who did not return your love, then you might consider the notion that you have been acting on this faulty assumption.

It is probably not possible to become an adult without having thought you loved someone and feeling that you were loved in return. Your love could have been a boyfriend or girlfriend, a lover, a friend, your parents, or other relatives. Sometimes, though, you were not loved in return. You may have shared secrets with your loved one, or invested a lot of time and energy in the relationship, only to find that your love was not reciprocated.

This probably resulted in what is called "narcissistic injury." This means that your essential self was hurt. No one recovers from a narcissistic injury easily or quickly, if ever. Indeed, as you read this, a particular relationship may come to mind that still has the power to evoke the hurt you experienced. As you read this, you may even be getting in touch with the hurt you experienced in many previous relationships. One possible cause for repeated experiences of this kind might be that you hold to the faulty assumption that you can feel worthwhile only if you have someone to love you.

Loving someone and being loved in return is indeed a wonderful experience. You may feel valued, inspired, uplifted, cared for, and a sense of happiness and joy. Loving and being loved contributes to meaning and purpose in life, to your well-being, and can even play a role in your physical health. The benefits of loving are numerous.

However, when loving is not reciprocal, there can be negative effects, with you ending up feeling diminished and flawed because you did not receive the love you gave, whether that person was a parent, friend, sibling, or lover. This is the outcome this book addresses, and your negative responses are likely to be based on the faulty assumption that all you have to do to be loved is to love the other person. If you cling to this basic and faulty assumption, even many incidents to the contrary will not allow you to change.

Love and Feeling Worthwhile

"I can only feel worthwhile if I have someone to love me." The key component in this faulty assumption is the word "only." If being loved is the only way you can feel worthwhile, then you are missing numerous opportunities to feel worthwhile, and may be missing the opportunity to love yourself, flaws and all. There are other ways to feel worthwhile besides being loved.

If you believe in this faulty assumption then you open yourself to being easily misled into thinking that you must have someone to love you, and you must do whatever it takes to keep that someone loving you. You may also have an erroneous impression that others blame you if you don't have someone to love you. You will find that you often misread and misinterpret others' intentions, tend to fall in love easily and to be continually disappointed. Moreover, it you think this state is limited to women, think again. Some men, too, cling to this faulty assumption.

Feeling worthwhile, cared for, valued, respected, and wanted are boosts to self-esteem. However, the foundation for your self-esteem lies in your early experiences and how you were treated by others from birth to the present. To a considerable extent, your self-perception is determined by your interactions with others in your world and is also influenced by your personality. One reason why this faulty assumption is difficult to overcome is that it has been internalized and acted upon throughout your life. It is, however, possible to modify it to the extent that it will no longer be the basis for your relationships.

You may need to examine your assumptions about feeling worthwhile. In addition to exploring the basis for holding to this faulty assumption by examining your family-of-origin relationships, you can build other ways to feel worthwhile. Self-esteem does not have to depend on being loved. You can find other ways to love and admire yourself. You should also reexamine your past relationships. You may have overlooked times when you were cared for and valued, but for some reason you dismissed them, or remained unaware.

Feeling Excited and Alive

"*I can feel alive and excited only when I'm with the person I love.*" Being with the one you love can be exciting and energizing, especially during the first stage of the relationship when you are finding out about each other. But if this is the only time when you feel this way, you are investing too much in that relationship, or person, may be expecting too much from him/her and are overlooking other possibilities for generating these good feelings. If you believe in this faulty assumption, you are too constricted in your life.

Do you feel "dead," empty, or fragmented when you are not with the one you love? If you miss the person, that's okay. But, if you have much very intense and negative feelings about yourself, that's not okay. These are the feelings that can lead you to act in ways that are not in your best self-interest, and may even be destructive. Others can find it easier to manipulate you to do what they want you to when you devalue yourself this way.

Can you remember a time in your life when you felt excited and alive without having to be with a special someone? Was there ever such a time? If there was such a time, you can revive and renew the activities that produced these feelings, e.g., dancing, sports, crafts, or volunteer activities to rebuild your energy and self-esteem. If there was never such a time, you will need to create and develop other experiences to produce excitement and energy, and explore your early experiences further to find what could have led to you feeling this way.

There are many ways to generate excitement and the sense of being fully alive. These paths are, of course, all personal to the individual and you will have to find those that best fit you. Here are some suggestions, derived from the professional literature:

- altruism

- spirituality

- esthetic sensibility

- creativity

- civic virtues and responsibility

Now that you have some sense of your emotional susceptibility and have begun to see how it impacts your life and your relationships, we will move to a discussion about how this susceptibility takes place and what you can do about it in the short and long terms.

Chapter 3

You Are Not Always
Responsible for Others

Boundaries are the defining parameters for physical, relational, and psychological limits. Boundaries are where we differentiate ourselves from everyone else. They are the borders where, as individuals, we end and others begin. To be aware of and understand personal boundaries require more than intellectual or cognitive perceptions; it requires a deep understanding of personal individuality, uniqueness, separateness, and an awareness of when these personal boundaries are violated.

Because much of this awareness takes place on a nonconscious or unconscious level, it is useful to obtain a better knowledge of your own boundaries if you wish to build or fortify boundaries that are not as strong and resilient as they might be. Furthermore, it is useful, where necessary, to develop differentiation. Differentiation is that aspect of your self-identity where you are aware of being apart from others, and that they are different and apart from you. This sounds simple, but many people do not fully understand that others are unique worthwhile individuals who are not under their control.

Types of Boundaries

Four types of psychological boundaries are discussed in this chapter: resilient, soft, inflexible, and spongy.

Resilient boundaries: People who have the capacity to adapt to different situations have resilient boundaries. That is, they can be strong when necessary and not allow their "self" be violated or intruded upon. If necessary, their boundaries can become inflexible to repel projections and projective identifications, but can also be flexible enough to open to permit the self to feel empathy for another.

Soft boundaries: People who have soft boundaries lack psychic strength. Their boundaries are fragile and can be easily subdued by others. Their self is constantly at risk of becoming enmeshed, overwhelmed, and/or manipulated by others.

Inflexible boundaries: Those who have inflexible boundaries are unyielding and rigid. These boundaries protect the self, but they are also armor that prevents the person from experiencing empathy. Such boundaries serve to keep the person isolated, alienated, and unable to make satisfying emotional connections with others.

Spongy boundaries: People who have spongy boundaries have some strength and can repel some projections and projective identifications, but their boundaries are also capable of being penetrated, usually without their knowledge or permission. Although it is possible for them to be open in some areas to allow some empathy to be experienced, their spongy boundaries can be so impenetrable that large parts of the self are closed to empathy.

Mark, a thirty-year-old married man with two young children and a very demanding job, was visiting his parents. They were both in their early sixties and still working. Mark tried to visit them at least once a week with his wife and children, but since both the children had colds and ear infections he had come alone this time.

Shortly after he arrived, his mother asked him when he had last visited his aunt who lived a couple of blocks nearby. Mark did not get along with this aunt, and avoided her when he could. When he told his mother that he had not visited his aunt, and did not intend to, his mother berated him for his attitude. She then said he should have brought his children to visit that day, so that he could take them to see his aunt.

Depending on the kind of boundaries he had, Mark would have reacted in one of four ways to deal with this situation. Here are some of the ways he would have reacted if he had had each of the different psychological boundaries being discussed.

Soft Boundaries

Mark immediately felt guilty, apologized for his attitude, and promised to go and get his children to take them for a visit to the aunt whom he disliked.

Inflexible Boundaries

Mark simply looked at his mother and told her again that he had no intention of either changing his attitude or visiting his aunt.

Spongy Boundaries

Mark felt a twinge of guilt at his mother's words as he knew how much her sister meant to her. He realized that his attitude toward his aunt was based on childhood experiences, but he still did not want to visit her. He lowered his eyes and promised his mother he would take the children to visit his aunt next week.

Resilient Boundaries

Mark told his mother that he understood why she wanted him to visit his aunt with his children, but they were sick and should not be disturbed. He acknowledged that he did not like his aunt but also said that he should not let his feelings about her affect his children's relationship with her. He promised to think about visiting her with the children.

Boundary Violations

This exploration of boundaries begins with an introduction to how you may be violating others' boundaries without even knowing what you are doing. In this way, you will gain a more personal understanding of how common boundary violation is, how unintentional some acts are, and how you may be as guilty as others of occasional acts and attitudes that are felt as intrusive. The following list of actions may increase your understanding of how your own boundaries may be violated, without any conscious awareness on your part that a violation has occurred.

How often do you engage in any of the following activities?

- Enter someone's office without knocking.
- Tell a friend that he/she ought to do something.
- Pat a child on the head.
- Hug a person without permission.
- Refuse to take "no" for an answer.
- Use a family member's possession without first asking permission.
- Accept a social engagement for a spouse, child, lover, or other intimate.
- Tell someone something that you feel they need to know "for their own good."
- Give phony compliments.
- Tell jokes with sexual implications.

These are common examples of violations of different boundaries. Reexamine this list to see if any of these experiences have happened to you and made you uncomfortable. For example, if a friend tells you that you "ought" to do something you don't wish to do, does that make you uncomfortable? If it does, your discomfort could arise from several different sources such as guilt, or not wanting to offend or anger your friend. For the moment, however, the source of your discomfort is not as important as the realization that the act does make you uncomfortable.

Physical Boundaries

Physical boundaries refer to the space around our bodies that we consider as "me" or "mine." This discussion focuses on the physical body and its extensions in space, such as when you are standing in a room. Physical space boundaries are:

1. *Intimate distance,* defined as eighteen inches extending around your body;

2. *Personal distance,* defined as eighteen inches to four feet around your body;

3. *Social distance,* defined as four feet to twelve feet around your body; and

4. *Public distance,* defined as more than twelve feet apart.

Intimate refers to close and personal space, such as that which feels comfortable to you when you are in a conversation with family, friends, and lovers. Personal distance refers to casual interactions, such as might take place at church, or at a supermarket. Social distance refers to *impersonal* interactions like job interviews, and public distance is everything more than twelve feet from your body, such as at a town meeting (Hall 1976). Violations of physical boundaries include the following:

- bodily abuse like beatings
- neglect that results in physical deprivation
- sexual violations
- touching without permission and inappropriate touching
- "cornering"
- using possessions without permission
- standing or leaning too closely to someone
- lack of respect for someone's privacy
- entering someone's room or space without notice or permission

Even some acts considered friendly or affectionate may be violations of physical boundaries. For example, hugs, pats, nudges, and other playful gestures are violations, when done without permission. Children are frequently touched by adults, especially affectionately, without their permission. Note that not all physical boundary violations are extremes like sexual abuse, rape, and beatings. Many boundary violations are thoughtless actions without conscious intent to harm, like patting a child on the head.

Unconscious acts of physical boundary violations play an important role in your emotional susceptibility, both violations you do and those done to you by others. For example, you may allow others to stand closer to you than you like, or you may accept unwanted hugs. You may accept these physical violations out of the misguided notion that it would be rude to object, or from the fear that you might offend the other person, and that it would be "wrong" to offend him or her.

However, acceptance of even playful and affectionate violations can be an invitation to others to make even more intrusive violations. Have you ever been unexpectedly kissed, accepted it, and then found that the other person moved to an even greater physical intimacy with you, such as caressing or fondling, and you did not want such physical intimacy at all?

By accepting the first violation you unintentionally conveyed the message that you might accept more intimate gestures. Although acceptance of a little bit does not mean a whole lot is okay, by not setting clear and firm limits on what you are willing to accept, or even on what you want, you allow others to misread your desires. If you are to block becoming enmeshed or overwhelmed with other people's emotions, you need a clear understanding of your comfort zones in the context of your personal physical boundaries. Some specific strategies to strengthen your understanding of acceptable boundaries are described later in this chapter and in chapter 4.

Relational Boundaries

It should be obvious that you have different boundaries for the various people with whom you interact and have relationships. However, some people, and you may be one, have some difficulty understanding this concept. In other words, you can tolerate and desire greater physical and psychological intimacy from those people in your life whom you feel close to, and tolerate and desire less intimacy from those who are progressively more distant in their relationship to you. O'Neil and Newbold (1994) define relational boundary violations as happening when "the interaction between two parties is not appropriate to the relationship" (57).

Some examples of relational boundary violations are as follows:

- taking advantage of the other person

- making demeaning, devaluing, and disrespectful remarks

- gossiping, criticizing, and being judgmental

- acting or speaking in a prejudiced, biased, or bigoted manner

- putting yourself first at all times

- acting in a codependent way

- manipulating or exploiting another

- having an attitude of entitlement

- harassing someone sexually or physically

All the acts and attitudes in this list are negative and you would want to work to eliminate any of these that reflect your behavior and attitudes. However, at this moment, your primary focus is on the acts and attitudes of others that are directed at you.

Look at the list again. How many of these behaviors do you encounter from your family, lovers, friends, and coworkers? Don't deny the impact such acts and/or attitudes have on you by rationalizing that the other person is just joking, doesn't mean you any harm, or that you have no choice but to endure such acts. Recognizing violations of your relational boundaries is an important component in understanding how to reduce your emotional susceptibility.

You may allow such violations because you desire the relationship so much that you are willing to endure these violations to maintain that particular relationship no matter how uncomfortable it might be. However, it is unlikely that this is the only relationship where you experience these violations. If you are experiencing such acts and attitudes from *many* different relationships, it's no wonder that you catch other people's feelings—because you have few or no relational boundaries.

See chapters 4 and 5 for strategies and guidelines on how to stop boundary violations, build stronger relational boundaries, and develop more satisfying relationships.

Psychological Boundaries

Psychological boundaries are the most difficult to describe as they are internal and unique to the individual. Your psychological boundary strength is also related to the extent to which you have achieved psychological separation and *individuation* (self-identity) from your mother or mother figure. (Note: Today, many fathers are their children's primary caretakers, and they fill the role of chief nurturer, or "mother" figure, in the family. Here, "mother" is used as a generic term, which includes fathers or anyone else who is the primary caretaker for a child or children.)

Narcissism is another aspect of development that impacts on one's psychological boundaries. *Narcissism* is commonly defined as an excessive self-love and self-focus, i.e., when a person is self-absorbed in almost everything he or she does or says. Age-appropriate narcissism means that the person has healthy narcissism for her or his age. Healthy age-appropriate narcissism is a critical component for strong psychological boundaries.

Having said all that, psychological boundaries are those that define the "self," i.e., a deep understanding of where you end, and an equally deep understanding of other people as distinct, different individuals. Those who do not have this understanding perceive others as extensions of self; and thus under their control to be ordered, manipulated, and used in the service of self.

Many of the boundary violations you experience result from the other person's incomplete understanding of this concept, as well as your own incomplete understanding of your own boundaries. Many boundary violations, and the acceptance of these violations, take place on the unconscious level, which makes it difficult to perceive and address them. Psychological boundaries can be seen in one's ability to:

- be appropriately assertive

- say "no" and stick to it

- express wishes and desires openly

- respect others' boundaries

- be appropriately empathic

- give and receive favors

- form and maintain satisfying relationships free of exploitation

Your psychological boundaries may be violated by a combination of external and internal forces operating together. That is, you may experience an external assault or intrusion, and because of *internal underdevelopment*, e.g., narcissism, you permit the violation. Internal underdevelopment can be seen in external acts or attitudes like the following. Do any of these describe you?

- The inability to say "no" and/or stick to it

- Easily offended and not shy about letting others know it

- Expecting others to read your mind and give you what you want or need

- An entitlement attitude (i.e., one that conveys a feeling of superiority and a suggestion that you should be treated as "special")

- Expecting others to do favors for you, but never doing favors in return

- Inability to accept favors from others

- Feeling exploited in many relationships

- Always putting others' needs before your own

- Getting lost or overwhelmed by others' feelings

- Expecting others to do exactly what you tell them to do

- Being easily hurt by what others say about you.

The chief focus of this book is about building and developing resilient and stronger psychological boundaries, as these will enable you to withstand the intrusions and assaults that lead to violations of your boundaries. The next section describes some fruitful areas to explore for personal growth and psychological development. At this point, you may be unaware of your undeveloped boundary strength, age-appropriate narcissism, and other factors that may be contributing to the violation of your psychological boundaries and to much of the distress you experience as a result of those violations.

You will also find in the next section some theoretical concepts to help you better understand how your boundaries may have failed to develop. These are psychological theories about the first few years of life, about what happens in the inner life of the child, and how the mother-child relationship has an impact on the child's later development, even into adulthood. These are theories, of course, because we have no way of accessing, assessing, or really knowing what goes on in a child's inner world during the pre-verbal and early verbal stages of human development. Children do not yet have the concepts or words needed to express their inner experiencing.

Boundary Development

The development of your boundaries begins when you are born and continues throughout life. The course of normal, expected, and healthy boundary development is tied to the sequence of the overall psychological development you experience. Margaret Mahler, a clinician who worked with and conducted research on mothers and their children, described one such sequence (Mahler, Pine, and Bergman 1975). That sequence has the following stages:

- Stage 1: The entire focus of the infant is on him/herself and personal needs. This stage lasts from birth to two months.

- Stage 2: The infant begins to recognize others but still has a strong personal focus. The infant perceives mother and self as being joined; this stage lasts from two months old to four or five months.

● Stage 3: The baby begins to explore his/her world, recognizes many others, and begins to form a concept of him/herself as a unique individual, separate from mother, but still requiring mother's emotional availability. This stage lasts from five months throughout one's life.

● Stage 3a: The child can physically separate self from mother without anxiety, but requires visual contact with mother.

● Stage 3b: The child can tolerate short periods of being separated from mother, but still expects mother to appear when wanted. The baby explores his/her surroundings and tries new activities.

● Stage 3c: Longer and longer periods of separation from mother are tolerated without the child feeling abandoned. The child begins to try new activities, experiencing both successes and failures.

● Stage 3d: The sense of being separate and the sense of the "self" as a different individual continue to emerge and become solidified. This period begins around eighteen months to two years, and the process of becoming separated and individuated continues throughout life.

This is a very brief summary of some of Mahler's theories about the stages of psychological growth and development. She, and other theorists and clinicians, believe that many emotional and relational disturbances have their basis either in the disruption or incompletion of one or more of these stages, especially stages 3a through 3c. Disruptions and incompletions result from various causes including neglect, abuse, abandonment, overprotectiveness, and underconcern. Whatever the cause, when the child fails to get what he/she needs during a particular developmental stage, that disrupts the process that would allow him/her to complete the sequence or stage successfully. Examples of disruption are as follow:

● maternal depression

● overprotective mother

● birth of a sibling

● severe poverty

● maternal substance abuse

● abrupt changes in the family's standard of living

● significant changes in family, e.g., divorce, elderly parents with crises such as health problems

Clearly, there are many situations that can arise in families that may prevent the child from receiving what he/she needs from the mother.

Kohut's work (1977) also provides some concepts for psychological development that are helpful to understand the course of psychological growth and development: these are mirroring, empathy, and healthy narcissism. Kohut believes that the pattern of lifelong psychological development, which begins in childhood, is significantly influenced by the *mother's reactions to her child*, and that there is healthy adult narcissism as well as healthy, age-appropriate narcissism in children and adolescents.

Mirroring

Mirroring occurs when the child's concept of self is reflected in the mother's face, attitude, and handling of his/her physical body. Babies have what is termed *grandiosity*, i.e., an inflated sense of self. If the grandiosity could be put into words, it might go something like, "I am wonderful!," "I am magnificent!," and "I am powerful." Kohut maintains that for healthy psychological development, this grandiosity must be mirrored by the mother who reflects, or mirrors, on her face, in her voice, and in her handling of the baby that she, too, considers the baby to be wonderful, magnificent, and powerful.

Empathy

As stated in chapter 1, empathy is the ability to enter the world of the other person and feel what he/she is feeling, *without losing your sense of "self"* in the process. Empathy is *not* becoming enmeshed or overwhelmed by the other person's feelings. The mother's ability to empathize with the child creates in the child a sense of security and confidence that his/her needs will be met, not ignored or minimized. This deep sense of security and confidence is basic to building strong boundaries. A mother's empathic responses to her child demonstrate that his/her welfare is important, he/she is valued, and he/she is deeply understood. Kohut maintains that disturbances and distress later in life stem, in part, from empathic failures experienced early in life.

As noted previously, healthy narcissism is age appropriate. Kohut describes *healthy adult narcissism* as characterized by creativity, humor, empathy, and wisdom. At all ages, narcissism is the perception, value, and love one has for one's self together with an appropriate recognition of others-in-the-world. Narcissism, as defined here, is primarily self-focus without being only self-absorbed. Although complete self-absorption is expected in infancy and childhood, age-appropriate narcissism reflects a gradual movement away from complete self-absorption and a recognition and respect for others.

Behaviors and attitudes reflective of age-inappropriate or underdeveloped narcissism in adults include the following:

- exercise need for attention

- admiration hunger

- entitlement attitude

- shallow emotional experiences and expressions

- lack of empathy

- a deep need to be considered unique and special

- exploiting others

- inability to form and/or maintain long-term satisfying relationships

Underdeveloped narcissism in the mother can play a significant role in the child's psychological development because she considers the child to be an extension of herself, and thus, under her control at all times. The child is neither allowed to follow the normal course of separating and individuating, nor does the child receive the resources needed to develop resilient, strong boundaries.

These concepts of mirroring, empathy, and narcissism are basic to understanding the next section, which discusses some of the possible reasons that you may not have developed strong boundaries. Remember, resilient, strong boundaries are necessary to provide shielding for yourself against "catching" others' emotions; while not damaging or losing your capacity to be empathic.

The Self-Absorbed Parent

Children require a lot of care, attention, and nurturing for their growth and development, and these needs continue over quite a few years. The usual expectation is that parents will have enough emotional maturity and healthy adult narcissism to be able to put their infant's and child's needs ahead of their own. Being a parent is not easy under the best of conditions. However, there are parents, like those described in *Children of the Self-Absorbed* (Brown 2001), who remain so self-absorbed that they:

- Do not put the child's needs ahead of their personal ones

- Consider the child as an extension of themselves

- Expect the child to be and do what they want them to be and do
- Consider it their right to manage every aspect of the child's life
- Crush any hint of independence in thought, action, or feeling by the child
- Use the child to obtain attention and/or admiration
- Do not express love or liking for the child
- Make the child responsible for their emotional well-being
- Do not empathize, or only rarely, empathize with the child

The self-absorbed parent usually has a considerable amount of underdeveloped narcissism that makes it impossible for him/her to meet the child/s needs, especially during the formative years where the child is also self-absorbed, demanding, and time-consuming. Under these circumstances, the normal course of the child's psychological development cannot be successfully completed. This is the parent who exhibits many of the following behaviors and attitudes toward her/his child:

- Criticizes and blames
- Makes demeaning and devaluing comments
- Withholds approval when parent's needs are not met
- Expects the child to know, i.e., read their mind regarding, what the parent wants and give it to him/her
- Does not empathize with the child
- Exploits the child to obtain status, attention, and/or admiration
- Is emotionally unavailable to the child
- Feels entitled to violate the child's boundaries
- Is capricious and arbitrary in many instances

These sorts of behaviors and attitudes have a very negative impact on the developing child's psychological growth. The mirroring and empathy that Kohut maintains as necessary for the development of the "cohesive self" simply does not take place.

How Were You Parented?

Now, take a moment and reflect on your memories of your parents, both of them, or, if you were raised by others, remember and reflect on them. Although the mother-child relationship may play the most significant role in psychological development, the impact of a self-absorbed father is also significant and must be considered. Reflect on each parent separately and answer the following questions. Your answers should be based on your feelings and perceptions.

Exercise 3.1: Were You Parented by a Self-Absorbed Parent?

Directions: Take a sheet of paper and write the numbers from 1 to 10 down the side of the sheet. Write "Mother" at the head of one column at the top of the page, and "Father" at the top of another column. Use the following scale to rate each parent separately:

1—Never, or almost never, did this.

2—Seldom did this.

3—Often did this.

4—Frequently did this.

5—Always, or almost always, did this.

Self-Absorbed Parent Scale

Using the scale above, answer how often your parent did or does the following:

1. Made you feel shame for not meeting expectations.

2. Blamed you for not being or acting as he/she wanted.

3. Was critical of your looks, dress, attitudes, opinions, and so forth.

4. Made demeaning comments about you.

5. Devalued you.

6. Said and did things to make you feel you could never be good enough to please him/her.

7. Did not seem to understand or care about your feelings.

8. Said or did things to hurt your feelings, and, if you protested, said you were overreacting.

9. Expected you to excel in academics, sports, music, etc., and claimed credit for your accomplishments and successes.

10. Was very upset if you did not "read their mind" and give them what they wanted.

Scoring Your Parent's Self-Absorption

Add the scores for each parent or parental figure. Use the following guide as an indication of the extent of self-absorption you perceive as characteristic of one or more parents.

0 to 19: Little or no self-absorption

20 to 39: Self-absorbed sometimes, but not often

40 to 59: Self-absorbed much of the time

60 to 79: Very self-absorbed

80 to 100: Extremely self-absorbed

If your scores for either parent was 60 or more, then you have some reason to believe that that parent had a considerable degree of underdeveloped narcissism, and that you did not receive the mirroring, empathy, and sufficient amounts of separation you needed in order to develop your own self-identity, and to develop resilient, strong boundaries.

The Parentified Child

The "parentified" child is one who has unconsciously and unknowingly assumed the responsibilities for the parent, usually the mother, from infancy on, and whose psychological growth and development were shaped by that experience. Note that the words *unconscious* and *unknowingly* are used. Neither the parent nor the child is consciously aware of what is taking place, i.e., the nurturing and caretaking roles are reversed.

Parental responsibilities include the following:

- Attending to the infant and child's emotional and psychological needs

- Helping the infant and child to learn how to manage emotions such as frustration and anxiety

- Understanding what the child wants and needs during the preverbal stage

- Care and nurturing of the child's physical, emotional, and psychological needs

- Being there when the child needs them, and so forth

Notice that all the responsibilities are one-way, i.e., the parent gives to the child. This is the usual and expected role for parents. When the roles are reversed, the child becomes "parentified," and, on a very deep level, is made to feel responsible for the emotional and psychological well-being of the parent. Think back for a moment. Did either of your parents frequently say any of these statements to you? Fill in the blanks for your particular experience:

- You are making me mad (upset, sad, etc.).

- Your actions shame me.

- Don't you care about my feelings?

- You're doing that just to annoy me.

- I love you when you do _____ .

- It makes me feel good when you _____ .

- Don't you want me to feel _____ ?

- If you loved me, you would _____ .

- If you loved me you would not_____ .

- You're getting on my nerves.

All of these and similar statements point the finger of blame at the child and either openly or indirectly, make the child responsible for how the parent feels. If you frequently heard these types of comments when you were growing up, you may be a parentified child.

Brown (2001) has described two responses of the parentified child: compliance and rebellion. That is, either the child becomes pliable and takes on the responsibility for the parent's well-being, or becomes defiant and refuses the responsibility. The former is seen as the "sweet" child and the latter as the "difficult" child. Neither develops resilient, strong boundaries. The compliant "sweet" child winds up with soft and/or spongy boundaries that open him/her to being very emotionally susceptible. The rebellious "difficult" child generally develops inflexible or spongy boundaries that keep out others' projections and projective identifications, but also keep him/her from accepting the empathy and other positive emotions directed at him/her.

The Emotionally/Physically Absent Parent

If you had one or more parents who were emotionally and/or physically absent during your formative years, you also may have difficulties with boundaries. It seems that when the mother is absent, the lasting effects are more significant than when the father is. There are many reasons why parents may be absent. These include the following:

- death

- depression

- severe emotional disturbance

- substance abuse and addiction

- work requirements

- hospitalization

- long-term illness

- military service

- incarceration

- divorce

- a chronic or acutely sick child who requires considerable attention and care

As you can see from this list, there are many reasons why a parent can unintentionally be emotionally and/or physically unavailable during the child's formative years. What is not included but also may be significant is the plight of the single parent who must work to earn a living and be a parent at the same time. Neither job is easy, both are time-consuming, and, sometimes, neither job can be done as well as the person wishes to do.

Although the parent's emotional maturity and underdeveloped narcissism may not be factors in why a child does not develop resilient, strong boundaries, being emotionally and/or physically absent can be a major factor. This is not to say that all children whose parents fit the descriptions in the list above will not develop strong, resilient boundaries. Many children do develop acceptable boundary strength in spite of their parents' lack of emotional maturity and underdeveloped narcissism. However, if you do not have such boundaries, and you had one or more parents who were emotionally and/or physically absent, both of those factors may have contributed to your "fuzzy" boundaries..

Family-of-Origin Contributions to Boundaries

- Were the children in your family allowed to have personal possessions that were theirs alone?

- Were possessions considered common property, to be shared by everyone, and were you sometimes scolded or punished if you did not want to share?

- Were closed doors respected by others, including parents, who knocked before entering your room?

- Did your siblings and/or parents respect your need for privacy?

● What were family expectations about touching?

● Did some forms of touching not feel right to you, but you accepted it?

● In your family, whose needs had priority, the children's or the parent's?

● Were the children expected to attend to the parent's emotional well-being?

● How were praise, encouragement, and approval handled in your family?

The answers to these questions provide some clues about the attitudes and behaviors in your family of origin that helped, or did not help, in the formation of your psychological boundaries. Others in your immediate world during those formative years also made contributions to the type of psychological boundaries you now have.

All families have expectations for appropriate behavior, even if these expectations are not openly known or expressed. These are some of the family's rules, and every member is expected to abide by these rules. Some rules can lead to inadequate boundary development, especially those that teach you that your boundaries are not to be respected. Other rules that lead to inadequate boundary development include those that do not:

● Permit you to set personal limits that will be backed up by authority, i.e., your parent

● Recognize and respect your need for privacy

● Allow you to reject undesired touching even though the touching may be affectionate

These rules and reactions are ingrained, acted on unconsciously, and are very difficult to recognize and change.

Exercise 3.2:
Were Your Boundaries Respected?

Take a few moments and complete the following exercise. You will need a sheet of paper and a pen or pencil.

Step 1. On the far right of the page create three columns. Write "Child," "Teen," and "Adult" at the top of the page as your column headings.

Step 2. Write the list of "family-of-origin behaviors" on the far left of the page. Your page should look like this:

List of Family-of-Origin Behavior   Child   Teen   Adult

List of Family-of-Origin Behaviors

1. I was frequently forced to share possessions.

2. I was made to feel guilty about not sharing.

3. I was told by a parent that I was selfish for not sharing.

4. A parent or sibling used my possessions without first asking permission.

5. Parents and/or siblings entered my room or space without knocking or notice.

6. My parent(s) did not respect my privacy.

7. I was expected to attend to my parent's emotional needs.

8. I was touched and/or hugged frequently, without notice, and I had to accept it even if I did not want or like it.

9. I was told that I was ungrateful, difficult, and so forth if I protested or pulled away from the touch.

10. I seemed to violate unspoken family rules often.

Step 3. After making the list, place a checkmark in each column where you experienced the action or feeling. Pay particular attention to the adult column as these are continuing family-of-origin behaviors and attitudes that are still having an impact on your boundary development today.

Step 4. Now, make two lists. The first list will be the behaviors and feelings that you can change immediately, such as insisting that others respect your privacy. The second should list the actions of others and your feelings that you will need more time to address adequately. The second list can be a part of the objectives you want to work on to reach your goal of resilient, strong boundaries.

Examples:

List 1

Insist that my possessions not be used without my permission.

Lock my bedroom doors.

Knock before I enter my sister's room.

Ask my father to borrow his tools. Don't just take them.

List 2

Learn to say no and not be coaxed into doing something I don't want to do.

Put my needs first sometimes, instead of my mother's.

If I don't want to be touched or hugged, I'll move away, or not get within touching range.

Development and Fortification

By now you may have a better understanding of the following issues:

- How your psychological boundaries are failing to protect you from external and internal assaults

- The extent of your emotional susceptibility

- How your early experiences played a role in the current state of your boundaries

You should have also formulated some objectives for developing strong, resilient boundaries. The desirable goal of strong, resilient boundaries will take some time to accomplish and you will experience some setbacks and failures. These are to be expected, but you must not become discouraged. You can and will make progress. Be patient and stay aware of even small victories. That will be supportive and encouraging.

The following chapters describe some techniques and strategies you can use to fortify your boundaries, and reduce or eliminate susceptibility to catching others' emotions. The personal work needed can be facilitated by working with a competent therapist who has the expertise to guide your individual exploration. The information in this book is of a generalized nature, although it is possible for you to individualize and personalize it for yourself.

Chapter 4

Let Others Have
Their Feelings

Sam was sitting in the family room when his wife came home from the PTA meeting very upset. He asked what was wrong and she spent the next twenty minutes telling him how the president of the PTA had ignored her suggestions, been contemptuous of her, and did not understand anything. As she talked, she became even more upset and angry, and Sam found that he too was becoming angry. He started pacing the floor, clenching his teeth, and balling his fists. As he became angrier, his wife calmed down. Sam "caught," identified with, and acted on his wife's anger.

In their book, *Emotional Contagion*, Hatfield, Cacioppo, and Rapson (1997) describe susceptible *receivers* of emotions as those who "have a psychological investment in others' welfare" (166). On the other hand, they describe *senders* as relatively insensitive and unresponsive to those who are responding to them. What seems to happen is that one person is open to the emotions of the other person, but the other person does not care about the open person.

To put this concept in personal terms, there may be instances where you may attend to and care about the other person's feelings, wants, desires, and/or needs while he/she is interested only in getting what is wanted, regardless of the cost to you. In such a case, your caring and concern is used against you.

Senders have some common characteristics that you may recognize. They are frequently:

- nonverbally expressive
- exploitive
- powerful projectors of emotions

- able to recognize and exploit vulnerability

- acting from strong power, control, and manipulative needs

- able to lie, mislead, or distort to get what is wanted

- relatively unempathic or unempathic

Nonverbal Expressiveness

Nonverbal behavior is thought to be more expressive of true feelings than verbal behavior in most human interactions, and it is said to carry 90 percent or more of true messages. Most nonverbal behavior takes place on the unconscious level, and both the person exhibiting the behavior and the observer send and receive the message on an unconscious level. This unconscious level makes it more difficult for you to be consciously aware of what is being acted out at the time it occurs.

Thus, the dynamics of what can happen are these: You may have a psychological investment in the other person; that person wants something from you; you are open to him/her and receive their nonconscious, nonverbal message on your unconscious level; *and* you then respond *unconsciously* to the message. The unconscious nature of the nonverbal communication and response may startle or surprise you and leave you bewildered about what happened.

The Dynamics of Nonverbal Communication

Let's try to examine what takes place on the nonverbal level. Because you already have a psychological investment in the other person, you are more likely to trust him/her and to feel that the two of you have some rapport. The types of relationships where psychological investment is expected to be mutual are these: parent-child, married partners, lovers, and relations between family members. These would be the strongest, closest, and most intimate relationships. You may have other relationships, e.g., friends, that are also characterized by your psychological investment in the person. The degree of trust and caring, of course, will depend on the particular relationship and the person.

When you trust someone and feel that there is mutual rapport, even when there is evidence to the contrary, this can mean that your nonverbal behavior communicates receptiveness. This receptiveness is indicated nonverbally in the following ways:

- making eye contact

- leaning forward

- orienting your body toward the other person

- mirroring the other person's posture

- holding your arms by your sides

- removing barriers between you, e.g., a sofa pillow, touching or allowing yourself to be touched

- concentrating visibly on what the person does or says

In this way, once you are attending to the other person nonverbally, you are then open to his/her projections and projective identifications.

Senders use nonverbal gestures, like those described below, that reflect their intent.

Gestures	Intent
Making eye contact	Establish connections, rapport
Standing or sitting close to you	Intimidation
Looming over you	Power and control over you
Touching you	Manipulation, seduction
Orienting his/her body toward you: "cornering"	Seduction, establishing rapport
Mirroring (reflecting your gestures and body positions)	Make you feel "in sync," merged, or enmeshed
Moving closer	Trapping, intimidating, controlling

In order to counter the sender's intent, you can increase your ability to recognize senders' nonverbal communication, identify your nonverbal receptive behaviors, and institute changes for your nonverbal postures and gestures. These can then become a part of your emotional shielding to make your messages more powerful and accurate. Specific suggestions and strategies are presented throughout this chapter.

The latter part of this chapter presents some specific strategies for recognizing senders' nonverbal communication, identifying your nonverbal receptive behaviors, and changes for your nonverbal postures and gestures that can become a part of your emotional shielding. Your messages can become more powerful and accurate.

Exploitation: Senders and Receivers

Some senders are underdeveloped narcissists (see chapter 3), which permits them to exploit others. Of course, they do not see it that way.

They are unaware and uncaring about their exploitive behavior, and consider it their right to manipulate others into doing whatever they want. It will be helpful to you to understand that these senders do not have much complete understanding of their own psychological boundaries, i.e., where they are separate and different from others. These people are still operating under the mistaken, infantile perception that other people are only extensions of themselves, and thus under their control. Children experience this a lot when their parents think of them as extensions of themselves.

These self-absorbed people are taking care of their "self" *at all times.* Even when they use words that seem to indicate an awareness of others-in-the-world, you need to be very aware that this is only a surface ploy, and it is done to accomplish something for their own good, not yours. All of their acts are in the service of the self.

This may be a difficult concept to accept. However, the extent to which you can reduce or eliminate your emotional susceptibility largely depends on your recognition that you are operating under faulty assumptions. You need to develop more realistic assumptions, e.g., senders are always looking out for themselves first and foremost.

One difficulty you may experience when trying to recognize and accept the truth that a particular person is exploiting you is that the exploitive person usually has some very engaging characteristics, e.g., he/she is charming, persuasive, and attentive. Such people can make you feel special, valued, lovely, and worthwhile, and these are wonderful feelings. For example, when your mother says something that makes you feel she loves you, you may feel uplifted, even though you know she is saying it to manipulate you. We all like these feelings and we are drawn to people who make us feel that way. However, if part of what happens in a relationship results in you feeling or being exploited, then you are paying too high a price for the wonderful feelings.

There are also senders who exploit other people by inducing feelings of guilt and/or shame in them. (Parents are very adept at this.) When you are involved with these senders, you wind up doing things you do not wish to do, and you feel exploited because you were told you "should" or "ought' to do those things. The induced guilt and shame results in you carrying out the sender's wishes.

Exploitation consists of both external and internal assaults. Someone wants something from you, and he/she does or says something that triggers an internal responsiveness within you, and you then act to provide the person with what is wanted. You must understand what your triggers are if your emotional shielding is to become effective. But, first, you need to recognize that the sender is exploitive, that he/she does not know that he/she is exploitive, and that this person generally feels that he/she has a right to use you and others in service to their "self."

Powerful Projectors

Some people are powerful projectors of emotions, and it can be very difficult to block the emotions they project, even when you are not in a relationship where you have a psychological investment in that person. For example, actors earn their living by projecting emotions to audiences. You have no connection with them, they are playing their roles, and you can still end up feeling the projected emotion. Children are also powerful projectors. The younger they are, the more powerful their projections can seem. If you are not shielded, you can easily feel the emotions that infants project.

The projectors in your life, however, who are cause for concern are neither actors nor children. The senders who are causing you distress are using their feelings to manipulate you into doing what they want you to do. You are not reacting out of your independent desire, you are feeling the brunt of that sender's feelings, and reacting to those feelings. Remember, for both of you, this manipulation takes place on the unconscious level. You are not consciously aware of his/her projections, and that person is not aware that he/she is projecting.

The more primitive emotions of fear and anger also tend to be the most powerful ones, and you are probably reacting to these most of the time. To illustrate, suppose you are with someone who is a powerful projector, and he/she wants you to do something, but is not sure you will cooperate. This person unconsciously feels that (1) he/she is entitled to get what is wanted; (2) has a right to expect and/or manipulate you to give what is wanted; and (3) is *fearful* of not getting the need met.

What can happen is that the sender's fear is projected onto you, and the sender then reacts to you as if you were fearful, e.g., moving closer, using a soothing voice, caressing or patting you to reassure you that you need not be frightened. You react to the fear by trying to "make it all better" by accepting the unwanted soothing and denying your real feelings, thus addressing the projected fear. If the sender can keep you from expressing fear, then he/she does not feel that fear, but you continue to carry the fear.

Your reaction and feelings are much more intense if you identify with any or all of the projected fear. You incorporate that fear, make it a part of yourself, and then become manipulated by it. This is another example of projective identification. Your psychological and physical boundaries have been violated and you are not consciously aware of the intrusion.

Exploiting Your Vulnerability

Other people can sense your vulnerability. Unknowingly you may send out signals that indicate you are available for manipulation and exploitation. I know that seems like a harsh statement, but it is important for you to increase your awareness of how you may contribute to some of your own distress. Your insecurity; lack of confidence; spongy, brittle, or soft psychological boundaries; your need for connections and reassurance; and your desire to be loved and valued put you in a position where others can sense that you are open to manipulation and exploitation. Add to this your conscious desires to be a caring, thoughtful, considerate, and sensitive person. Such desires are commendable, but not helpful in your present circumstances.

What are some of the signals you transmit that help the senders to sense your vulnerability? They might be nonverbal behaviors such as these:

- fingers in your mouth

- shifting eye contact

- slumping posture

- entering a room tentatively and looking around

- holding your body closed in on itself

- speaking in a very soft voice

- smiling at everything, everyone, or a lot

Some verbal indicators you might use that indicate your vulnerability are these:

- using qualifiers that make what you say tentative and unsure

- being indecisive

- raising your voice at the end of sentences, which makes it seem as if you're asking questions instead of making statements

- seeking others' approval

- not asking for what you want, but waiting for it to be provided for you

- agreeing to keep the peace

- talking about failed relationships

It may be pleasurable to be liked for being seen as shy and sweet, but the same characteristics that indicate shyness and sweetness are often seen as vulnerabilities.

Power, Control, and Manipulation Needs

Three different types of power and control needs are discussed here: they are coercion, reward or reinforcement, and referent. Coercion relies on threats, intimidation, and other use of force to exert power. Reward or reinforcement uses the promise of real or psychological goodies to exert power. Negative reinforcement, i.e., the threat of withdrawing something of value, also falls into this category. Referent power is that power you bestow on the other person. That is, you decide that the person has status, charisma, or a powerful personality, and your perceptions give that person the power that can then be used to manipulate you. For example, in high school, the status awarded to the captain of the football team and to the Homecoming Queen give them referent power. Both their positions and the perceptions of others give them power. The process used to get what you want from others, which involves the use of one or more power and control strategies, is called manipulation.

Coercion is easy to understand as a power behavior. The other person is forced in some way to do what is wanted. Force can be any of the following: persuasive arguments, appeals to one's desire to be cooperative or liked, group and peer pressure, and the use of physical force and verbal threats. If you respond to any of these, you will want to make your objective eliminating your openness to being coerced.

Reward or reinforcement power uses tangible and/or fantasized goods and services to gain what is wanted and to manipulate others. Positive reinforcement is putting something in, like a present or promise of future goodies. Negative reinforcement is taking away something desirable that is believed to be present like affection or financial support. Your responses to such power plays illustrate your needs and vulnerability. If you are fearful of losing someone's attention or affection, you will respond by giving that person what he/she wants. The same is true if you are desirous or needy of attention or affection.

Review your current and past relationships of concern, and note which ones are distinguished by power and control as their salient characteristics, especially those where you were coerced. Power and control are especially characteristic of many family relationships.

You will want to examine your particular needs that made you susceptible to the power and control needs of others. You will also want to examine those relationships where you bestowed power upon the other person.

Lies, Distortions, and Misleading Statements

Senders make considerable use of lies, distortions, and misleading statements to manipulate you and others. These people do not have any sense that their dishonesty is morally wrong; they are just "doing what everyone else does." Many of their lies are of the variety called "white lies" or "sweet lies," where the sender's intent is to make you feel good. When you feel good, you are more likely to appreciate him/her and do what he/she wants you to do. Many people consider lies like these harmless. They do not realize the negative impact such lies may have.

You, and some senders, may engage in flattery, insincere comments, compliments, and other verbal acts that are less than honest. This is not to propose that you should always be brutally honest. "Brutal," by definition, can be very hurtful. This is just an attempt to show you that you, too, act in this way, and there is seldom any malicious intent. You do not set out to hurt the other person. A sender, however, may feel the same way consciously, but, unconsciously, may want to manipulate you for personal gain.

Making yourself immune to flattery is certainly one way to stop being manipulated. Needing to hear flattery, compliments, or "sweet lies," e.g., "I could never love anyone but you. You're the only one for me," contributes to your emotional susceptibility. Do you respond to statements like the following by feeling valued, pleasured, or appreciated?

- No one understands me like you do.

- You're the most beautiful (handsome) person in the world.

- I don't think I can live without you.

- You're a better daughter (son) than your siblings.

- Just looking at you makes me feel good.

- You've got something no one else has, and I like it.

- You give me something no one else can give.

- You understand me in a way that no one else does.

There are relationships where any of the above statements is a true expression of feeling. What you must learn is how to distinguish when such statements are "sweet lies," and when they are honest feelings. This is not always easy to do. Your need to be flattered, complimented, and told "sweet lies" should be a part of your self-examination.

You cannot stop others from lying, distorting, and making misleading comments. What you can do is to better understand the psychic payoff when you hear such comments. This deeper understanding of your own responses can lead to being able to distinguish between white lies and an honest expression of feelings, and lessen your need for flattery and compliments. You can reduce your tendency to be manipulated significantly by increasing your understanding of your need to be flattered.

Lack of Empathy

It can be hard to accept that anyone is insensitive to your feelings. However, senders tend to lack empathy, and until you can accept them as they are, i.e., insensitive to your feelings, you will not make much headway in developing emotional shielding, and you will stay open to "catching" their feelings.

You may find it difficult to see senders as they really are because you make the faulty assumption that they are, in many respects, like you. After all, there is support for the idea that we feel understood by people with whom we share common characteristics (Rogers 1975; Brown 1989). Since you probably consider yourself as a caring, considerate person who is sensitive to others' feelings, you may operate on the unconscious assumption that the people in your world, or those to whom you are attracted, are similar to you in this respect. This assumption will be one of the most difficult fantasies you have to overcome.

You probably have ample evidence that some people in whom you have a psychological investment are insensitive to your feelings and/or the impact their behavior has on you (people like your parents, siblings, and other family members). Yet you continue to expect them to change, any minute now. But they do not change. They continue to be insensitive. These are the people who:

- Push you to do what they want

- Refuse to accept "no" for an answer

- Don't recognize when you are upset

- Change the subject if you try to talk about your feelings

- Redirect all conversations to focus on themselves

- Use all the right words, but the feelings behind the words are absent

- Have an essential coldness at their core

- Are ruthless in pursuit of what they want

- Feel entitled to have what they want, regardless of the cost to others

You may be defending yourself from recognizing their insensitivity by rationalizing, repressing, or denying both the person's behavior and its impact on you. Nothing you can do or say will cause this person to change. Nothing. If the person changes, it will occur because he/she perceives that changes are needed and desired. The only constructive acts you can take are to work on yourself: build resilient, strong boundaries, develop emotional shielding, and engage in a more realistic appraisal of the people in your world and your acceptance of them.

Shielding Against External Forces

Building a shield against external forces will take some effort and require you to make some changes in your habits. There are very effective nonverbal and verbal strategies to help repel emotional assaults from others, protect you from their projections, and give you more time to work on your shielding from internal assaults. As you read through the next section, select the strategies you feel are in accord with your personality. When you first begin using any of these, you will probably become uncomfortable, but stay with your plan. At some point, your discomfort will cease. Your goal of building strong, resilient boundaries begins here.

Exercise 4.1: Your First Shield

Materials: Felt markers, crayons, or colored pencils; two large sheets of paper 18 inches x 24 inches.

Procedure:

1. Sit in a quiet private place with a desk or table for drawing. Close your eyes and imagine you have a shield in front of you. Notice every detail about the shield on both sides, the side facing you and the side facing out. Observe the height, length, width, density, the material from which it is made, color, decoration, etc. This shield can protect you from others' emotions and projections, and is being developed for you.

2. Imagine how far the shield is from you. Is it six inches or closer? Further than six inches? Is it touching your body? Where is it?

3. When you have a good picture of your shield in your mind, open your eyes and draw it on the first sheet of paper, noting as many details as possible.

4. On the second sheet of paper, draw a picture of yourself with your shield in place. Try to place the shield the same distance from your drawn figure as you imagined the distance when your eyes were closed.

Look at both pictures. You can recall these anytime you need to remind yourself to put your shield in place. Be patient. There will be times you will forget to use the shielding, or remember it only after someone has ignored or breached your boundaries. The trick is to learn to raise your shield *before* the emotional assault and/or violation takes place. That will take time, practice, and conscious thought.

This exercise is entitled "Your First Shield" because there is more work to be done to fortify this shield, and to build strong, resilient boundaries for yourself. For a first step and for the short term this shield will suffice.

Nonverbal Strategies

There are nonverbal strategies that can be more easily instituted than anything else, and when used judiciously, they will allow you to make more independent and objective decisions. You can lessen the effect of others' emotions and projections on you when your nonverbal behavior gives you the space to move away, and the time to think instead of feel, to analyze and evaluate what is happening. Your actions then can be guided by careful consideration of your options rather than by impulsive reactions to emotions.

Changing your nonverbal behavior can be very powerful since the nonverbal component of messages is the most accurate. One reason you have been the target of others' emotions and projections is that you nonverbally convey receptivity and vulnerability. Here are two exercises to increase your awareness of your unconscious nonverbal communication.

Exercise 4.2: Reflections

Materials: Full-length mirror and photographs of yourself in social and/or family gatherings.

Procedure:

Stand in front of the full-length mirror and note the following:

- your posture

- your arms' position

- your legs' position

- your head position, i.e., erect, slumped, held back

- your facial expression

What do you notice about your posture? Are you slumped over? Open? Is your chest out? Are your hips thrust forward?

Are your arms folded across your chest? Or do they hang down by your side? Clasped behind your back? Does one arm hold the other?

Are your legs pressed together? Are they further apart than eight inches ? Is one leg behind the other? Are your knees locked or relaxed?

Is your head pushed forward, chin jutting out? Or is your head slumped forward with your chin pointed toward your chest? Is your head held back with your chin sticking out? Do you hold your head erect?

Finally, what is your facial expression? Are you smiling? Frowning? Looking shy and tentative? Is this your usual expression when you're with someone?

The second part of this exercise uses the photographs. You can examine them one by one, or spread them out on a table. Either way, look at yourself in the pictures and focus on the same aspects of nonverbal communication used to examine your reflection in the mirror in the first part of this exercise, e.g., your body posture, arms, and legs' positions, facial expression, and so forth.

Now, put your two sets of observations together and write a short summary of how you may be communicating receptivity and vulnerability.

Exercise 4.3: Personal Space

Materials: Full-length mirror

Procedure: This exercise can be completed alone using just your imagination and the mirror, or with the help of a friend. It is designed to increase your awareness of your intimate, personal, and social space, or distance, zones. (See chapter 3.)

Using a Mirror

Stand in front of a full-length mirror, about six feet away. Imagine that the reflection you see is that of a stranger. Begin walking toward the stranger and stop when you start to feel some discomfort, even a slight discomfort. Note how close you are to the stranger at this point.

Next, stand about six feet away and imagine the stranger walking toward you. Note how far she is from you when you begin to feel some discomfort. The distances in these two instances are estimates of your *social* space zone. Try to fix the physical distances where you begin to experience discomfort in your mind as a reference point to use in the future for how physically close you can allow others before you move away.

With a Friend

Have your friend pretend to be a stranger. This is called *role play*. Stand about six feet apart and begin walking toward each other. Both you and your friend should stop walking when you say, "Stop." Look into each other's eyes as you approach. Keep trying to imagine that your friend is a stranger. Note the amount of physical distance between the two of you when you say, "Stop."

Repeat the procedure except that, this time, you will recognize your friend as your friend. Again, note the physical distance between the two of you when you say, "Stop."

The differences between the distances in these two activities provide estimates of your comfortable social and intimate space zones. Of course, it can be quite difficult to imagine your friend as a stranger; on some level, you continue to recognize her/him as your friend. That is why these distances are only estimates.

Variations on Exercise 4.3

1. Imagine the stranger (friend) is of the same sex as yourself.

2. Imagine the stranger (friend) is of the opposite sex.

3. Imagine the stranger (friend) is very attractive.

4. Imagine the stranger (friend) as looking dangerous.

5. Change the stranger (friend) to be younger, older, of a particular racial/ethnic group, and so forth.

Now that you are more aware of your social and intimate space zones, try to move them *back* six to twelve inches. This move back will be only temporary. When you are better fortified, you can allow people to get physically closer to you. The reason for moving your intimate and social zones back is that, when others are physically close to you, you may not have the psychological boundaries to keep from "catching" their emotions and projections.

Two Sets of Shields

You are building two sets of emotional shielding so that, *at your discretion,* you can allow others to get close to you, and so that, in the event your outer level of shielding is breached, you will have a second level of shielding to keep you from becoming enmeshed or overwhelmed. This second set will be very helpful with family members and friends whom you may not be able to move back out of your personal zone, but from whom you need emotional shielding.

The second set of shielding is formed internally and is discussed in chapter 5. This set takes longer to understand and to develop because it is unique and individually created for you alone. In this chapter we are concerned with the outer or external shielding that is more general and is focused on some observable behaviors.

Incorporating Nonverbal Strategies into Your Shield

You have begun to build your external shielding. You now have some ideas about where your personal and intimate comfort zones are located, an image of your personal shield, and some sense of how your body and gestures may communicate receptivity. You have received some suggestions, e.g., moving your social and intimate zones further back, and many more suggestions are forthcoming.

However, before suggesting additional strategies, let's take a look at the circumstances where you most often become enmeshed or overwhelmed by others' emotions. There are numerous situations where this might happen, and it can be helpful for you to understand better where and when you seem to be most vulnerable.

- Do you become enmeshed or overwhelmed quickly and without warning?

- Do you realize only gradually that you are enmeshed or overwhelmed?

- Is it only after evidence of betrayal, abuse, or other insensitive acts that you accept that you are enmeshed or overwhelmed?

- Are you ever warned by others that you are letting someone get too close, or that you are being manipulated, but you don't see the relationship that way?

- Are you convinced that you can help the other person?

- Do you wake up one day and realize that you've become enmeshed and/or overwhelmed again?

- Are you readily available as a "shoulder to cry on"?

- Do you want to see the good in everyone so much that you ignore or overlook behavior and attitudes to the contrary?

The first two questions may provide some guidance for short-term strategies you can use. If the "catching" of emotions and projections happens quickly, you will want to examine the settings where this occurs. For example, does it generally happen in social situations where you are trying to have a good time, and you are not on guard? Social situations can be especially vulnerable places and times, as can family gatherings. You are generally sociable and outgoing during these times, willing to overlook or deny any concerns you may have about a relationship, and this leaves you open and receptive to "catching" emotions and projections. Understanding where and when you are vulnerable can help you become more aware of staying shielded.

If the "catching" of emotions and projections happens over time, and you become aware of it only gradually, the strategies you would use are different than when the "catching" is quick. You would need a blend of external and internal shielding to deal with a gradual awareness, whereas quick "catching" can be addressed with external shielding only. However, even when your awareness is gradual, you can use external shielding to give yourself the space and time you need to reflect on what is happening, your responses, and possible pitfalls.

Nonverbal Shielding Against Quick "Catching"

The following section presents some nonverbal strategies you can use to shield against the quick "catching" of others' emotions and projections. Review these first to determine whether you do the opposite behaviors, such as making eye contact. Then, read the list as a cluster of gestures and behaviors to be instituted almost in their entirety, at first. As you gain stronger, more resilient boundaries, you can relax using some of these clusters, for you will have a better understanding of when to allow yourself to become connected, and to whom.

- Do not attend to the other person.

- Do not sustain eye contact; look at the person's nose or forehead.

- Move away ever so slightly.

- Restrict smiling or mirroring the other's facial expression.

- Entwine your legs.

- Look around the room.

- Visualize somewhere else, e.g., a place of peace.

- Don't preen, i.e., don't stroke yourself, nor fiddle with your hair or jewelry.

Do not give the other person your full attention or act interested in what he/she says to the exclusion of anyone or anything else in the area. Look around, turn your head away, orient your body away from the person as if you are leaving or inviting others to join you. If standing, move back a few inches; if sitting do the same or put something, like a purse, between you. If you have to look at the person, restrict your smiling or mirroring of his/her emotions and do not maintain eye contact.

Suppose you have an uncle who always tells you all of his woes in exhausting detail, and you end up "catching" his feelings. You like your uncle, but you want to stop catching his emotions. Think about your physical stance, your posture, etc., when you tend to "catch" his feelings. You probably stand close to him, your body turned (oriented) toward him, sustain eye contact, and your facial expression is sympathetic or similar to his. To stop catching his emotions, you can alter your physical stance as described above. These body and facial shifts do not have to be major changes; even minor adjustments will help.

Let's try a harder situation. You suddenly realize that your aunt is well on her way to seducing you to do something you do not want to do. What she specifically wants you to do is not as important as the fact that you do not want to do it. Your thoughts and feelings are confused and complex because you want to maintain the relationship, please her, and not arouse her anger or your guilt, but you don't want to do whatever it is that she wants you to do. The discussion about internal forces (see chapter 6) will try to address your thoughts, feelings, faulty assumptions, and so on. As noted before, these are more difficult to address. The focus here is only on extracting you from the situation so that you do not wind up doing something you do not want to do.

If you follow the behavior described above and physically move back, break off eye contact, stop mirroring her facial expression, and repeat to yourself, "I don't have to do anything I don't want to do," you can disassociate yourself. Unfortunately, your aunt will most likely be the type of person who continues to push to get her way, regardless of what your nonverbal behavior may be communicating. You may need to give up your fantasy of being subtle and become more direct, i.e., move further away. Visualizing your external shield also will be helpful.

Verbal Strategies

Your nonverbal behavior will be more effective when combined with one or more of the following verbal behaviors.

- Do not explain or become defensive.

- Do not respond.

- Do not argue.

- Use a clipped, strong voice.

- Use titles and be formal when addressing the other person.

- Say "No" and leave, hang up, etc.

- Tell the person that you don't appreciate his/her attempts to manipulate you.

- Propose that you and the other person be "friends." (This is a less than direct way of saying that you recognize the person's attempts at manipulation or seduction, but you are not receptive.)

- Say, "Get away from me!" if a less direct approach fails. This is unlikely to be misunderstood.

Not responding is classified under verbal strategies because various ways of nonresponding are used that relate only to verbal exchanges. That is, the person who is trying to seduce, manipulate, and/or intimidate you is using words, and your tendency may be to respond to words with more words. You may have the erroneous idea that you have an obligation to respond to whatever is said to you. You do not. You have no obligation to reply, explain, argue, or defend your position. Too often, when you respond, you only provide another opportunity to the sender to send you emotions or projections that you can then "catch."

If you are in the habit of using a soft, quiet voice, try to save that voice for special people and for special occasions. Speak in a clear, decisive voice that is moderately soft. You can always soften your tone to sound "sweet," "sexy," or soothing. It's much harder to raise your voice after starting to speak softly. A strong voice conveys confidence, self-assurance, and sends the message that you intend to take care of yourself.

Do not remain in the other person's presence after you say "no." Say it clearly and firmly, then leave; or, if on the telephone, hang up. Staying available gives the person another opportunity to try to change your mind, or it may convey the message that you are ambivalent, and that some possibility exists for you to change your mind. Whether you are right, wrong, or indifferent about saying "no," when you do say it, stick with it.

There are more aggressive verbal strategies to use if you need them. These illustrate going on the offensive. For example, you can tell the other person that you recognize what is happening, and you do not like it. You may receive the response that your perception is wrong, but the person will back away. In addition, you will have indicated a strong sense of your boundary. That is always a good thing to do.

At first, these strategies may seem rude to you, and you may have some reluctance to use them. However, if you are not being respected by the other person, you are the only one who can save yourself. You needn't be rude, but there are some people who get the message only when faced with an aggressive statement.

Blend Verbal and Nonverbal Strategies

The third set of strategies is a blend of verbal and nonverbal approaches. This set includes behaviors and attitudes such as the following:

- Do not discuss your personal concerns.

- Hear only meaningless noise.

- Do not request favors.

- Visualize the person in a comical or undignified situation.

- Be indifferent.

When you discuss your personal concerns, you tend to focus on your feelings about them, thus leaving you vulnerable and open to "catching" others' feelings. You can become mired in either positive or negative feelings and forget to maintain your boundaries. You are self-absorbed at this point; others can use your distraction to project their feelings, and your defenses are not in place to prevent you from "catching" them.

You may yearn for comfort and reassurance, and because the other person is saying what you want to hear, you make the faulty assumption that he/she cares about you. What the other person perceives is a golden opportunity to seduce or manipulate you. Be very selective about the people with whom you share your personal concerns, and try never to share personal concerns in social situations.

I once saw a cartoon that showed a man talking to a cat. The man was telling the cat that her behavior (the cat's) was unacceptable. The balloon above the cat's head indicated that what the cat heard was gibberish—meaningless sounds. Yes, the cat was attentive, but kitty didn't hear or understand one word. Trying to imitate a cat and not hearing or understanding what a sender says to you can be a very effective strategy.

Do not ask others to do favors for you except when to do so is unavoidable. Make sure you really need whatever is requested, and do without whenever possible. When others do us favors, there is an implied or a direct expectation that we are then under an obligation to return the favor.

There are people in this world who prey on others by doing favors for them and thus making them feel obligated. Such favors never seem to be adequately repaid. And such people never let you forget that they did a favor for you. If you do favors for others, let them be gifts with no expectation of payback.

When you start to feel that you are "catching" emotions or projections you can pull yourself back from being caught by visualizing the other person in a comical situation. Visualize the person in situations such as these: dressed in a clown's costume or wearing a dunce's hat; stuck in an undignified pose like receiving a pie in the face; and so forth. It's hard to catch an emotion or projection when you are secretly laughing inside.

Indifference is a powerful tool against "catching" emotions and projections. Indifference is like a dense gray fog that nothing can penetrate. You simply do not care. It is not your concern or problem and you have no intention of trying to "fix it," neither are you going to do anything to try to make the other person feel better. Learn how to act indifferently even when you do not feel indifferent. When your internal shield is better fortified, you will *be* able to be appropriately indifferent in reality. Care when you want to, but do not care to the point where you become enmeshed or overwhelmed by others' emotions.

Chapter 5

How You Play into Others' Hands

The focus for this chapter will be on methods for developing your shield against some of your internal forces, such as your faulty assumptions and beliefs about yourself, and the major source for these faulty assumptions, i.e., old parental messages. From the time you are born, your self-esteem, self-perception, self-confidence, and self-efficacy are significantly influenced by the perceptions and reactions others have toward you. These perceptions and reactions interact with your personality characteristics and life experiences to produce the way you view yourself. We begin with an exercise on self-perception.

Exercise 5.1: Me

Materials: A sheet of paper and a writing instrument, e.g., pencil or pen

Procedure:

Sit in silence and think about how you perceive yourself at this moment. Let mental pictures of yourself emerge as images, feelings, symbols, and so forth. Don't edit or change what comes up for you. Do this for about five minutes. If you feel yourself drifting away, or becoming mired in feelings or memories, stop and begin the next part of the exercise.

Respond to each of the following terms with a personal statement about yourself. Begin each statement with: *I am*. (Examples: Under "Looks," you could write *I am handsome*. Under "Failing" you could write *I am failing at my job*. Under "Talents" you could write *I am talented at dancing*.)

Looks	Sexuality	Worth and value
Failing	Succeeding	Sex role
Abilities	Talents	Character
Morals	Health	

Read back what you wrote and note how many positive statements and how many critical or negative statements there were.

These statements are the beginnings for your self-exploration of some of your faulty assumptions, beliefs about yourself that may not be realistic, and the degree to which you are still negatively influenced by your old parental messages.

Old Parental Messages

Do not underestimate the continuing impact of the messages you received as a child from your parents and others in your world. You were continually bombarded with spoken, unspoken, nonverbal, conscious, and unconscious messages that you rejected or accepted. Those you accepted you incorporated as part of your self without conscious intent. These messages continue to exert major influences on your feelings, behavior, attitudes, and self-perceptions in direct and hidden ways. Such messages can be very important reasons why you did not develop sufficient boundary strength, and why you are open to "catching" others' emotions.

Do you remember your mother doing any of the following?

● Criticizing you for not meeting her expectations

● Blaming you for not being different than you were, e.g., like someone else

● Making demeaning or devaluing comments about your decisions, choices, opinions, etc.

● Making sarcastic comments about you

● Poking fun at you

Or, were there more times when she did the following?

● Standing up for you when others criticized or blamed you

● Saying comforting things when others made demeaning and devaluing remarks about you

● Complimenting you on how you looked, or on something you did

● Looking at you and smiling as if she were pleased to see you

● Making it clear to others that she was in charge of your welfare—not them

Now, go back over the two lists and substitute your father for your mother. Which set of messages were most prominent for your parents, the negative ones or the positive ones?

The negative messages also may have carried some hidden statements about your essential self that you may have incorporated and that are still influencing your behaviors, attitudes, and self-perceptions today. Instead of your parent(s) saying these things about you, you say them to yourself. For example:

- Do you blame yourself when something goes awry?
- Do you emphasize how you fail rather than focusing on your successes?
- Are you afraid to admit mistakes?
- Do you hide behind a mask and fear the real you becoming known to others?
- Do you yearn for someone to care for, soothe, or protect you?
- Does the slightest hint of criticism deeply hurt you?
- Do you laugh at yourself because others expect it, or so that you will be perceived as a good sport?
- Are you constantly trying to please others, and do you feel like a failure if they are not satisfied?

The list of residual feelings, behaviors, attitudes, and self-perceptions can be very long. Understanding what old parental messages still influence your self-perception can help you to understand your current circumstances when you are open to catching others' emotions. What can happen is your old parental negative messages can be easily triggered and, on some level, you revert back to your younger self and behave as you did then; however, when this occurs, you remain unaware or unconscious of what is happening.

To illustrate this point, suppose that you are asked to do something, and you do not want to do it. Your reluctance will show, even though you haven't openly said "no." The other person then:

- Talks about how much it would mean to him/her for you to do it
- Has an earnest expression on his/her face
- Talks in an intense way that signals how much emotional investment he/she has in your answer
- You then "catch" that person's emotions
- You begin to feel guilty about failing to meet his/her needs or expectations, just as you did with your parents
- You berate yourself for not agreeing to do what you do not want to do, or you do agree to do what you do not want to do

What you heard and felt, on a nonconscious level, were your parents' old messages that criticized and blamed you. Your guilt was aroused, and you acted as you did with your parents: you agreed to do something you did not want to do. It did not make any difference that the current circumstance differed in significant ways from those you experienced as a child with your parents; for example:

- The relationship was not as significant

- You were not under any obligation to meet the other person's needs or expectations

- That which he/she wanted you to do was not necessarily in your best interest

- You still felt guilt and acted on it

Other people, especially senders, capitalize on triggering old parental messages to arouse guilt and shame. Messages about you like the following can trigger guilt and shame easily:

- being ungrateful

- being unappreciative

- losing love and affection

- not being good enough

- causing parental emotional distress

- making parents feel ashamed

- being fatally flawed, etc.

To make these feelings go away, you give the sender what he/she wants.

Faulty Assumptions

Exercise 5.2 presents some common faulty assumptions. Indicate the extent to which you easily can think or feel that way, using the designated scale.

Exercise 5.2: My Faulty Assumptions

Materials: A sheet of paper and a writing instrument

Procedure: On a blank piece of paper number from 1 to 10 on the left side of the page. Answer each of the following as:

1—Very difficult for me to think or feel that way.

2—Difficult for me to think or feel that way.

3—Easy for me to think or feel that way.

4—Very easy for me to think or feel that way.

5—Extremely easy for me to think or feel that way.

1. When I'm rejected, it's because I am inadequate or flawed.

2. I want (need) approval and acceptance from almost everyone.

3. I have a responsibility to live up to others' expectations.

4. I would be wrong not to feel responsible for other people's happiness.

5. I must not fail to please others.

6. Others are like me and have the same needs and desires I do.

7. Others will love me if they think I am worthy of their love.

8. I need to listen to others because they know better than I do what's good for me.

9. If someone asks me to do something, it would be mean and unkind to refuse to do it.

10. Pleasing others means that I am loved.

Scoring: Add your rating for each item to get a total score. Scores range from 10 to 50.

40–50: You find it extremely easy to buy into these faulty assumptions.

30–39: You find it very easy to buy into these faulty assumptions.

20–29: You find it easy to sometimes buy into these faulty assumptions.

10–19: You don't have much trouble rejecting these faulty assumptions.

Rejection

If you immediately assume that something is wrong with you when you experience rejection, you are well on your way to triggering feelings of shame. Shame for not being any of the following:

- better
- more competent
- more lovable
- better looking
- shaped more appealingly

- more affluent

- talented

- smarter, and so forth

You can name your own list of flaws that you think may cause the other person not to want you. Even if you try to shrug the rejection off and/or place the blame on the other person, you keep coming back to the thought, "If I were better, he/she would not have rejected me."

Your essential or core self is hurt by this rejection, and you blame yourself. This self-blame is a product of the old parental messages that pointed out your flaws. You bought into these old messages (i.e., incorporated them), and they are easily triggered.

Approval and Acceptance

You may consciously know that approval and acceptance from almost everyone is an unrealistic expectation—a fantasy. You may even be able to verbalize this. However, your feelings and actions communicate the opposite when you do and say things dedicated to gaining others' approval and acceptance at the cost of your personal well-being, morals, ethics, and values. This is a big price to pay.

The lifelong yearning you have for love and acceptance from one or both parents may be at the center of your need for acceptance and approval from almost everyone. You grew up not having, or not being sure you had, your parent(s)' love and acceptance. Some of you may even have grown up with the full knowledge that you did *not* have your parent(s)' love and acceptance, because the parent(s) found one or more ways to reject you, such as engaging in these behaviors:

- abandoning you

- telling you he/she did not love you

- physically abusing you

- neglecting you

- emotionally abusing you

No matter how much you may have done to overcome early rejection or abuse, no matter how much you may deny that you still yearn for the unavailable parent's love and acceptance, some part of you still holds on to the fantasy that you can obtain that parent's love and approval. Now that you are older, this yearning gets played out with others when you work hard to obtain approval and acceptance from almost everyone.

Others' Expectations

The way we learn what behaviors our families and the larger culture expect of us is by the positive reinforcement we receive for meeting others' expectations, and the punishment and negative reinforcement we get when expectations are not met. We also learn behaviors by observing what others do, the responses they get for doing what they do, and by trial and error. This learning seems to be a lifelong process. It's known as *acculturation*, and every time we move to a different region, community, or country, some new learning is needed.

What was probably instilled in you from an early age is the faulty assumption that you are under an obligation to meet others' expectations, and you are wrong or flawed if you do not meet these expectations, or if you choose not to meet them. Even if you were given the message that it was okay not to meet some people's expectations some of the time, you probably were not provided guidance for deciding whose expectations to meet, or not to meet.

Such ambivalence and confusion may have led to a kind of paralysis or shutdown, and you just may have adopted the attitude that you had an obligation to meet others' expectations. If that was the case, you may be continuing to do things you do not want to do because someone else expected you to do them in the past, and you feel guilty when you do not meet expectations, even unrealistic ones.

Others' Happiness

You have neither the power nor the responsibility to make others happy, no matter what the relationship is. Happiness is individualistic and each of us chooses to be happy or unhappy. Yes, there are events and circumstances that contribute to feeling happy or unhappy, but it isn't the event or another person that causes either feeling, it's what we choose to feel about the event or circumstance.

You are not responsible for others' feelings, just as they are not responsible for yours. You may not have learned how to take responsibility for your personal feelings and may still look to others to "make" you feel positive. You may still become angry or upset when others "make" you have negative feelings. Believing that others "make" you have feelings is a faulty assumption, and believing that you "make" others have their feelings is also faulty.

Doing and saying things that provide you and others with pleasure is certainly desirable under most circumstances. However, if you feel that you have to take care of others' happiness and that you are wrong when you do not, this assumption can work to your detriment. Give others the responsibility to take care of their own happiness, and you take care of yours.

Pleasing Others

You can work yourself endlessly trying to please others, only to fail. Part of the reason you might fail is that you are working so hard to please that you do not recognize what you are doing is ineffective, i.e., the other person is not pleased. Such failures can trigger old parental messages that you are inadequate; then you feel guilty and ashamed.

Many people who have these feelings redouble their efforts to please others. What wasn't working becomes the basis for intensifying efforts and that, too, fails. The underlying issues are the old parental messages and the triggered feelings. You do not have to always please others, nor does your failure to please mean that you are flawed. The internal acceptance of this truth is not easy to achieve, but such acceptance is a necessary step in forming strong, resilient internal boundaries.

Others Are Like Me

There are many similarities among people, and we tend to choose to associate with those whom we consider most similar to us. However, this can be a very faulty assumption that leads us astray, i.e., that others are like us. Even when there are considerable similarities in background, interests, abilities, and so forth, there are also significant differences, and many of these differences are never discussed. They just never seem to emerge. So, we go on our way with the faulty assumption that because someone is like us in a particular way, he/she is like us in other ways.

There may also be similarities in needs and desires, but they differ in levels and intensities. For example, you may have a need to be independent and your sister may have the same need. However, the same need for independence may be played out very differently as your need for independence is more intense, or less intensive, than your sister's is. You can make big mistakes by assuming that others have the same needs and desires that you do.

For example, let's assume that you have the desire to be honest. The other person may have the same desire, but he/she may define honesty differently than you do, i.e., he/she may feel that one needn't be overly honest when it causes problems. That person may consider it honest to tell "sweet lies." You both would say that you value honesty, but you would have very different expectations for how honesty should be expressed.

Being Worthy

Being a good person is a desirable goal. Being loved is also a desirable goal. Feeling that only worthy people are loved is a faulty assumption, however; and feeling that if you are not loved, then you are not worthy, is another faulty assumption. What may happen is that you do everything in your power to be a good and worthy person, but you do not receive the love you feel you deserve. Or, when you don't receive the love you want, you decide that you must not be worthy—otherwise you would have the love you want.

Nothing could be further from the truth. Some very good and worthy people never find the love they seek. Furthermore, some not so good, or unworthy, people are able to find the love they desire. Being loved doesn't have much to do with whether or not you are a worthy person.

Old parental messages can be the basis for this faulty assumption. That is, your parent(s) may have given you messages when you were growing up that you had to prove yourself worthy of their love. On some occasions their love may have been withheld, and you were told that you were not worthy of their love. On the other hand, you might *never* have been told that your parents loved you—no matter how hard you tried to be and do what they wanted. If either situation was the case, you may still be trying to obtain your parent(s)' love through the love of other people in your life.

Listening to Others

Listening to others can be helpful. Others may have information, expertise, and/or life experiences that you can use for your benefit. However, it is a faulty assumption that we should listen to others because they know what's best for us—better than we do. Others can and do know some things better than we do, but there are no hard and fast rules for who these people are, or when they are on target or are in error.

During your childhood, you may have been told "listen to your elders," "your parents know best," and/or others "know more than you do." Some of you even may have followed that advice. Some of you may have made it a point never to listen to others. Both behaviors may have continued into adulthood where you "always" listen to others, or "never" listen to others. In neither instance have you learned how to make constructive use of others' experiences, knowledge, and understanding.

You do not have to listen to others and they do not know better than you do what's best for you, but there may be useful information others have for you if you allow yourself to hear it. You can cultivate an inner wisdom that allows you to hear what others have to say, sort through it, decide what is useful or true for you, and be in charge of knowing and deciding what is best for you.

Refusals

If anyone asks you to do something in such a way that you would be put on the spot if you were to refuse, this is a clear signal that you are being manipulated. If words are spoken with the intent of making you feel mean, petty, rude, or unkind for refusing, that person is trying to manipulate you. Requests for favors are honest when the person is open to allowing you to refuse without arousing these negative feelings.

There may be times when you experience such feelings because of *your* issues, not because the person phrased the request in a way that implied you were wrong or insensitive. Under the best of circumstances, you may have mild feelings of regret, guilt, and so forth., but these would be *your own* responses to your inability to do whatever was requested—*not* the result of someone's effort to manipulate you.

The old parental messages you carry have many possible outcomes. For example, even now as an adult you are doing some of the following:

- Working hard to please others

- Asking "what will the neighbors think" as a guide for your behavior

- Always taking care of others, and putting their needs ahead of your own

- Needing people to like you

- Believing that you should be cooperative, no matter how your principles are violated

- Helping those in need

Your parents may have manipulated you in the same way that others do now. You may be giving in to their manipulations without understanding that, on an unconscious level, you may still be trying to please your parents. Learn to sort out what you want to do from what someone else wants you to do, and do only those things you decide independently to do. Until you become more accustomed to practicing this behavior, you may have to live with some uncomfortable feelings for a while, but those feelings will moderate, or disappear in time. Eventually, you will be able to say "no" without feeling guilty. You will then be less susceptible to others' manipulations and feel better about yourself.

Being Loved

Allowing yourself to be manipulated to do things you do not want to do, or that are not in your best interest, for the sake of pleasing others, so that you will be loved, is counterproductive. The more you do, the more others will take advantage of you, and the less you will feel loved. Yet, you may continue on this unproductive path because of your faulty assumption that pleasing others equals or leads to those others loving you. The assumption is faulty because what you are doing did not work before, is not working now, and will not work in the future. No amount of your effort can make it work.

The ideal situation for babies is that they should be loved by their parents just as they are, unconditionally and completely. When babies and children experience this kind of love, they grow up secure and confident in knowing who they are, that they are lovable. They grow up without feeling that they must please others to be loved.

Some babies and children do not receive this unconditional love. The outcome of such an upbringing can be an adult who is still trying to form a self-identity, does not experience that he/she is lovable, and still yearns for the parental love he/she did not receive as a child. Such adults can spend considerable time and effort trying to get the love they yearn for by pleasing others. Their fantasy is that, if they please someone, that someone will love them. This may or may not happen, but their search goes on because of their underlying yearning.

The Impact of Assumptions, Beliefs, and Messages

What feelings are aroused as you read this chapter? Do you see yourself in what has been presented; i.e., do you hold negative beliefs about yourself and faulty assumptions? Do you continue to be influenced by old parental messages? If you do, then there are significant ways in which these influences are having a negative impact on your internal emotional shielding. In spite of this, you can learn to strengthen your internal emotional shielding. With the aid of adequate internal shielding your external shield then can become more powerful and constructive.

How does this work? When you employ your external shield to block others' feelings and projections it can be more beneficial for you if you do not have to feel your own negative emotions, i.e., guilt, shame, fear, and anger as responses to the other person. Also, your emotions become less likely to be triggered. If your feelings are not triggered, then the other person cannot manipulate you via these feelings. Together, both shields will prevent you from "catching" others' feelings and projections.

It can be helpful to make an estimate of the impact of the negative self-beliefs, faulty assumptions, and old parental messages on your self-perception, self-esteem, emotional susceptibility, and the quality of your current relationships. Use this scale:

1 = almost no or no impact

2 = a mild impact

3 = a modest impact

4 = a significant impact

5 = a considerable impact

	Negative Self-Beliefs	**Faulty Assumptions**	**Old Parental Messages**
Self-perception	_____	_____	_____
Self-esteem	_____	_____	_____
Emotional susceptibility	_____	_____	_____
Current relationship	_____	_____	_____

Which negative self-belief, faulty assumption, or old parental message has the most impact, e.g., the highest rating? This area can be your starting point for building a better internal shield. For example, if faulty assumptions are having the most impact on self-perception, this is the first area you would want to address.

Deciphering old parental messages will take time and effort as many of these messages are not readily available to the conscious mind. Some messages may be disguised, and you may be well defended against becoming aware of them. The rest of this book stresses personal development, and as you work through the exercises, some of your old messages may become more evident.

It is not necessary to know and understand all of your negative, old parental messages to make significant progress in developing your internal shielding and building strong, resilient boundaries. You can begin to reduce your emotional susceptibility and promote your personal psychological growth and development by using some of the suggested strategies, e.g., visualizing your external shield.

Some strategies that can help with strengthening your internal shielding are these:

- Become aware of your faulty assumptions

- Engage in constant mental monitoring

- Analyze your perceptions

- Shut off some of your sensitivity to others

- Distance yourself from others for the short-term

- Engage in positive self-talk and self-affirmations

Each strategy named above will be discussed and described but you will have to adapt or modify them to be consistent with your personality. This is not a "one size fits all" formula. These strategies can serve as a mental checklist to monitor your behavior and reinforce your internal shield. You also may want to experiment with some new behaviors, even though they are not consistent with how you view yourself at this time. You may be pleasantly surprised at the outcome.

Awareness

Thus far there has been considerable discussion and emphasis on faulty assumptions, and you are probably aware of just which ones influence your beliefs, attitudes, feelings, and behavior. You may even have many false assumptions, not just one or two. Although it can be painful to reflect on how you have allowed these assumptions to lead you into being emotionally susceptible, and into doing things you do not want to do, such self-reflection can be very beneficial. Your task is to be self-reflective, not any of the following:

● evaluative

● judgmental

● self-blaming

● self-critical

You can spend a lot of unproductive time on "should have," "could have," or "ought to." Berating yourself is *easy*, and because it is painful, it becomes easier to suppress, deny, and/or repress the old material and your current feelings. The intent of this self-reflection is to increase your awareness so you can better use what you know about yourself and your faulty assumptions when you encounter similar circumstances, situations, and people in the future.

Exercise 5.3: Awareness Building

Materials: A sheet of paper and a writing instrument

Procedure:

Sit in silence. Close your eyes if you wish to, but closed eyes are not necessary. Allow an event to emerge when you felt you were "catching" the other person's feelings. Try to use an event where you did not like the outcome of the interaction, for example, when you did something you did not want to do.

As you recall the sequence of events, try to pinpoint what you were reacting to or thinking about at the time. It is always helpful to identify the specific faulty assumption that was in play at the time; so try to label your thoughts, for example, "I can't be rude." If there were several faulty assumptions, try to let all of them emerge.

After reflecting and identifying one or more faulty assumptions, write them down. Repeat the exercise for three or four other events to get a good idea of the primary false assumptions that are triggered for you. These are the assumptions you will want to stay consciously aware of and use as questions for yourself, when you feel you may be in danger of becoming enmeshed or overwhelmed by others' emotions. Mentally ask yourself while you are interacting with the other person whether you are operating from a specific faulty assumption.

Mental Monitoring

Thinking can be a very powerful strategy and you may have to practice thinking rather than your usual response of feeling or acting. There are people who tend to become engaged, touched, or responsive through their feelings first. Others may act first and then feel or think, and some must think first, before their feelings or actions kick in. If you are emotionally susceptible, you are likely to have your feelings touched first. That's how others, e.g., senders, are able to engage and manipulate you. The same can be true if you tend to act first. Your habitual way of becoming engaged, being touched, or responding needs modifying. You don't want to lose the positive benefits of your usual mode, but you do want to learn how to use your capacity to think to a greater advantage.

"*What am I doing?*" and "*Why am I doing this?*" are the two questions that comprise mental monitoring. Staying in touch with what is happening at the moment is harder than it sounds, especially if you are more used to feeling and/or acting. You have to make a conscious effort to think. Using your external shield gives you some space and time to think about what is happening and what your responses are, but you still have to deliberately ask yourself these two questions.

Exercise 5.4: Mental Monitoring

Materials: Notebook and writing instrument

Procedure: Do the following for one week; on a daily basis, write about the awareness and the outcomes you achieve in your notebook. You can get more out of this exercise if you do it for longer than a week, but try to create at least one week of such entries.

1. Each day select one person with whom you interact to practice mental monitoring. Select interactions with someone whose feelings you do not tend to "catch." You may, if you want to, use a child or family member whose feelings you don't mind "catching." Work relationships also provide another good source for practicing this mental monitoring.

2. Each time you interact with the person, make a conscious effort to mentally ask yourself the two questions, "What am I doing?" and "Why am I doing this?" Note your responses each time.

3. Write a brief summary each day about the event, the answers to your questions, and the outcomes, i.e., what you did when you arrived at the answers to your two questions.

4. At the end of the week, read over all your entries and become aware of your mental monitoring and the amount of effort expended. What did you have to do to remember to ask the questions? Were there some events where mental monitoring was easier or more difficult?

5. Repeat the exercise with another person. Practice until you can slip into asking yourself these questions easily.

Analyze Your Reactions

Whenever there is an event, you have some sort of reaction. We are constantly reacting to external and internal events every day. But we may not be aware of the reaction, or if it is very mild or fleeting, we may overlook it. The process that follows illustrates how you can become more aware of what you are experiencing at all times, and that awareness can help you employ your external and internal emotional shielding.

1. The first step is to identify your reaction by labeling or describing what you are experiencing. For example, your reaction could be identified as: pleasure, fright, dismay, irritation, or feeling like you just want to get out of there. The important thing is that you give the experience substance and form with thoughts and words.

2. The second step is to make associations between the event and your reactions. What similarities are there between the current event and a past event, previous situations, people you've known and/or other relationships? The associations may be strong, mild, or scant. Much of the time you will see a continuing thread or cord of similarity. It's just not readily evident.

3. The third step is to identify and label the characteristics that the current experience has with past experiences. What are the specific similarities for the person, situation, event, etc.? It may be understandable that you might be reacting at this point, in part, to these similarities, rather than being objective about your current experience. For example, you may see some similar characteristics between this person and a beloved sibling. This may lead you to magnify the positives about this person, and to ignore or overlook major negatives about him/her.

4. The fourth and final step is to consider the possible implications of your reaction. You could be projecting your needs, wants, or desires onto the person, and reacting to them as if they had what you wanted, etc. You could be fantasizing that the person was your ideal, or cared deeply for you. You could be reacting to this person as if he/she were someone from your past. You don't have to do all of this at once, but you will find it illuminating to practice analyzing your reactions.

Sensitivity

There will come a time when you can allow yourself to be sensitive to others' feelings. That time will be *after* you have developed stronger, more resilient boundaries, and have sufficient emotional shielding so that you can better judge when it is safe to be sensitive to others. Until you reach that time or point, you can help reduce the negative impact of your emotional susceptibility by shutting down some of your sensitivity.

Shutting down means:

● Becoming more indifferent to and/or realistic about your responsibility for others

● Realizing that you are limited in what you can do

● Accepting that you have better uses for your emotional energy

● Allowing others to take responsibility for their own welfare

● Focusing on your well-being more often, but not exclusively

● Becoming more self-reliant

In short, you will become less emotionally available than you were. Your basic sensitivity will still be intact, but you will not let others have access to it as their needs dictate.

Distancing Yourself

Shutting down may not be enough to prevent you from "catching" others' emotions. You may need to employ some distancing techniques while you are building and fortifying your self. You need space and time to work on your boundaries.

Distancing is physical and observable, it is also psychological and felt. Physical distancing techniques like those described in chapter 4 can be helpful. Techniques such as pushing back your social and intimate zones, not maintaining eye contact, and putting barriers between you and others will send clear messages to others to "keep their distance."

Psychological distancing uses techniques such as the following:

- zoning out
- changing the subject
- making a joke
- visualizing a barrier between you and the other person
- not exchanging personal information
- limiting conversations to safe topics
- bringing others into the conversation
- not responding to seductive, provocative, or emotionally laden comments, and so forth

You probably know other such techniques. Just reflect on what someone does or says that keeps a psychological distance between you and him/her. Use those or some variation of them. There are many ways to promote psychological distance.

Positive Self-Talk and Self-Affirmation

The key to your internal shielding is positive self-perception, and one part of staying positive or becoming positive is your attitude about your strengths, weaknesses, successes, and failures. For example, you may feel relatively positive about yourself, but when you feel guilty or fail to live up to your expectations, you may blame or criticize yourself for not being "better." Your internal perception of how you "ought" to be is, in part, a product of old parental messages, but some part of it is under your conscious control and can be modified.

There is a big difference between taking responsibility and self-blame. The former is a desirable characteristic where you accept your actions. However, there does not have to be criticism attached to accepting responsibility. You intend to do better next time, or to take steps to prevent it from happening again. Self-blame is involved when you chastise yourself for not being powerful enough to have prevented the event, or not having had enough control of yourself or others. You assume that you alone have responsibility and control, and that you are flawed, bad, or wrong when things do not work out as you wished they would.

Assuming responsibility is realistic and adult. Self-blame is not realistic. It is judgmental and not adult. That said, there are exceptions, e.g., where blaming yourself can be appropriate. These, however, are extreme circumstances and you should be careful not to accept unwarranted blame.

The intent in this discussion is to point out the value of positive self-talk and affirmations, i.e., what you say and think about yourself, either silently or spoken aloud. The following exercise can help you develop your positive self-talk and affirmations.

Exercise 5.5: The Positive Me

Materials: A 3- x 5-inch card and a writing instrument

Procedure: Write "I am" at the top of the card on one side. Under that, write a list of five to six positive traits and characteristics that describe you. Some traits to consider including (if true for you) are these: kind, neat, organized, caring, tolerant, respectful of the rights of others. Do not include physical characteristics like tall or thin.

On the other side of the card, write "I can" at the top and finish that with five to six things you can do. For example, cook, dance, garden, or sew.

Read your card and put it where you can review it often, at least once a week. Expand your lists as you become aware of other positive things about yourself. These are your positive self-talk and affirmations. Remind yourself daily or weekly of what they are and substitute them every time you think something negative about yourself, blame yourself, or criticize yourself.

Chapter 6

Psychological Strength

The focus now shifts to discussions and exercises that can help you build your psychological "self." These are the longer-term strategies that will help you avoid "catching" others' emotions, or being easily manipulated by others via your identification with their emotions. These strategies also can help you in making independent decisions about what you do and do not want to do.

In chapters 4 and 5, you were given some effective short-term strategies to use and you were encouraged to practice them every chance you get. You were also encouraged to mentally formulate a checklist of your behaviors and thoughts as parts of your external and internal shields. This checklist will be most valuable if you can remember to use it *before* interactions. Using it during an interaction can be helpful, especially if you are feeling uncomfortable, but using it after an interaction is not helpful for that particular event, although it can be helpful to use as a reminder for the next interaction.

Your Psychological Self

Defining or describing a psychological self is not easy because it involves complex, abstract concepts that describe internal processes unique to each individual. The perspective used here uses these concept of *healthy adult narcissism* as its basic description of the psychological self, although other concepts, such as separation and individuation, are also present. The framework this chapter and later chapters provide is a guide for the following activities:

- Developing your personal underdeveloped narcissism

- Enhancing your appropriate emotional expression

- Expanding your creative and inspirational resources

- Developing deeper, more satisfying relationships

These are the inner resources that will enable you to be empathic without becoming enmeshed or overwhelmed, to make better and more conscious decisions about opening yourself to others' emotions, and to prevent you from being manipulated by others.

This part of the journey begins with a self-assessment about the current status of your healthy adult narcissism.

Exercise 6.1: My Self-Assessment

Materials: A sheet of paper and a writing instrument

Procedure: Rate yourself on the following characteristics using this scale:

1—Very low

2—Moderately low

3—High

4—Moderately high

5—Very high

1. I need to be the center of attention.

2. I need to be liked and admired by everyone or almost everyone.

3. I have a tendency to become enmeshed in others' emotions.

4. I have a tendency to become overwhelmed by others' emotions.

5. I wish to be treated as unique and special.

6. I am convinced that what I do or say can make "the" difference for another person.

7. I wish to have others do what I want them to do.

8. I feel that others have the secret to happiness.

9. I envy others their achievements, possessions, and/or relationships.

10. I want to be associated with people I consider of higher status, e.g., richer, more talented, better looking, etc.

Scoring

The items rated 4 or 5 are the behaviors and attitudes you will want to give the highest priority to understanding, and perhaps to modify. You will find it helpful to read and work through the material about items you rated 1–3, as you may not be fully aware of some of your behaviors and attitudes that reflect these aspects of underdeveloped narcissism.

The behaviors and attitudes in exercise 6.1 are descriptive of some aspects of underdeveloped narcissism; that is, the extent to which you have not fully developed age-appropriate adult narcissism. These aspects of self usually are not known to the person. He/she remains unaware that they have not developed this aspect of self, and this underdevelopment plays an important role in their ability to form and maintain satisfying relationships. The exercises and discussions that follow are intended to increase your awareness of your underdeveloped narcissism, and to provide you with specific behaviors and attitudes that can serve as guides for changes. That is, if you are doing, thinking, or feeling a particular way that reflects some aspect of underdeveloped narcissism.

You will then have a specific behavior, attitude, feeling, or thought to work on changing. For example, it isn't particularly helpful to know that you have a considerable need for attention. It is helpful when you know some actions you can take to change and reduce your attention-seeking behaviors.

Center of Attention

There is nothing wrong with liking attention. Receiving attention can make you feel special, valued, and cared for. These are all very positive feelings and their importance is not to be minimized. These are the feelings you may be seeking or may receive from your attention-seeking behavior. However, you are probably not aware that you are looking for attention to fill this need. You are most likely unaware that you are doing or saying things that call attention to yourself, nor are you aware of *why* you want or need constant attention.

There are many ways to get and remain in the spotlight. Rate how often you do each of the following:

1—Never or almost never

2—Sometimes

3—Frequently

4—Very often

5—Almost always

Attention-Seeking Scale

1. I arrive late to events.

2. I wear clothes designed to attract attention, e.g., flashy, tight, colorful, etc.

3. I talk and laugh loudly when in public.

4. I tell jokes and share gossip.

5. I make sure my experiences are told in detail.

6. I talk about my problems or difficulties every chance I get.

7. I interrupt others or finish their sentences.

8. I buy possessions so that others will notice them or be envious.

9. I mention myself in almost every conversation.

10. I table hop at restaurants or social events.

Scoring

Add your ratings. If your total score is 40–50, you constantly do things to call attention to yourself. Scores between 30–39 indicate that you often seek the spotlight. Scores between 20–29 indicate attention-seeking behavior on occasion, but not often. And scores below 20 indicate little or none of this behavior.

It is difficult to draw the line between excessive attention-seeking behavior and that behavior which is not excessive. Try the following exercise for one day to get some idea of the extent of your attention-seeking behavior.

Exercise 6.2: Looking for Attention

Procedure: For one entire day, pay attention to every conversation or interaction you have with everyone, including telephone calls and e-mail exchanges. Keep a running tally of the number of interactions where the focus was on you, or turned to you at some point. For example, if you had ten conversations, how many of these ten had some attention on you, your concerns, etc. It does not make any difference how brief the interaction or conversation was; the important thing is this: Did it relate at all to you in some way?

Another estimate that can be illuminating is to try to tally the number of times during the day that the conversation or interaction focused on you. That is, you may have had only ten interactions, but there were twenty-five times all told that the focus was on you.

The other tally that can help in determining your attention-seeking behavior is to note how often you initiate turning the focus to yourself and your concerns. For example, suppose you are having a discussion with someone who is facing surgery. He is talking about the seriousness of the operation and the chances that it will not help his condition. Your response is to say that you sympathize with him because you remember how you felt when you had to visit someone in the hospital. You say that you just hate hospitals. The conversation then turns to other things you hate—like being sick. The attention is now on you and your concerns.

Exercise 6.2 can provide you with some notion of the extent of your need for attention. Everyone wants and needs some attention some of the time. That's okay. If you become aware that your need is excessive, considerable, or in any way excessive, you may want to work on changing your behavior.

Changing your behavior will take some conscious thought about what you are doing. Why you have attention-seeking needs is not something that can be adequately addressed here, as the antecedents lie in your early experiences. Here, the major emphasis is on your behavior and on increasing your awareness of what you are doing.

Getting started on changes is relatively easy. Just look at the items on the "Attention-Seeking Scale," select those you rated 3 or higher, and begin to notice when you do them. It is at this point that you can consciously start to change the behavior, e.g., go to lunch at your usual place, but do not table hop. Stay in touch with your feelings as you try out the changed behavior, and try to tolerate the discomfort. The more you practice the changed behavior, the less discomfort you will feel.

The attention-seeking behaviors thus far have been active ones. There is also a set of passive attention-seeking behaviors. Rate how often you engage in these behaviors using the scale: 1 – almost never or never; 2 – sometimes; 3 – frequently; 4 – very often; 5 – almost always.

Passive Attention-Seeking Scale

1. I sulk when I don't get my way or I am not pleased with what someone is doing.

2. I stay or become quiet to avoid saying what I really think or feel.

3. I wait to be asked to become involved or to give my opinion.

4. I say, "Don't worry about me," but I don't really mean it.

5. I put an upset or distressed look on my face, but when asked about it, I minimize or deny feeling that way.

6. I stay away or withdraw when I don't get what I want, but I resist all attempts to draw me back into the situation.

7. I ignore someone, instead of working out conflicts or differences of opinion.

8. I become angry, express it, and refuse to let go of it, no matter how much others try to explain, accommodate, harmonize, make up, etc.

9. I make self-depreciating comments.

10. I speak very softly, so that others have to strain to hear what I am saying.

These passive ways of getting attention are as effective as the active ones. Repeat the process both for scoring and for beginning to change your behavior, as described for the more active attention-seeking behaviors. These passive behaviors can be more destructive to relationships, so you will want to give any behavior that you rated 3 or higher your immediate attention. You may be unaware that you are acting in ways that are detrimental to your valued relationships. Your scores on this scale can be your wake-up call.

Enmeshed and/or Overwhelmed

Although this entire book is focused on understanding and changing tendencies to become enmeshed or overwhelmed by others' emotions, one part of creating change is to expand your awareness of the part of your psychological self that participates in your becoming susceptible to others' emotions. There are many parts that make up the psychological self, and it is not easy to determine which aspect is involved, or in need of greater development. That is the main reason this presentation takes a broad brush approach.

So far, you've become more aware of the nonverbal messages you are sending, responding to, and perhaps misunderstanding. You've also been presented with an array of possible old parental messages that still may be influencing you, although you are now an adult. You have some information that can help you identify if, and when, unconscious associations with past experiences with parents and others are a part of "catching" others' emotions.

All this new information and greater awareness are part of strengthening your psychological self, developing your boundaries to become stronger and more resilient, and reducing your tendency to become enmeshed or overwhelmed by others' emotions.

This tendency also has an aspect that reflects the extent to which you have developed a self-identity separate and distinct from your parent(s). Not a superficial separation and individuation where you live apart and do much of what you want to do—the self-identity referred to here is a deeper psychological separation where you actively explore options and possibilities for such matters as the following:

- beliefs
- attitudes
- values
- career choice
- behavior

● opinions

● lifestyle

Exploring these matters leads you to making conscious choices about who you are, what you want to do and to believe, and how you wish to lead your life. You will not just drift into the way you are, you will make conscious decisions. For example, you will have a set of values that reflect what you consider to be right and good, not because your parents or society deemed these to be your values. The values you choose may end up being the same values as those of your parents and/or society, but you will decide whether to adhere to them, and not do so because they were imposed or incorporated without your awareness of what you were choosing.

The Difference Between Enmeshment and Being Overwhelmed

There is a difference between becoming enmeshed and overwhelmed, although the outcomes are similar. When you become enmeshed, you get pulled into other people's emotions. They pull and entice you into the storm they are experiencing. If you become enmeshed, you tend to get too close to others, perhaps in an effort to get the closeness you once experienced or still yearn for from your parent(s).

Becoming *overwhelmed* means that your attempts to stay outside the emotional storm are ineffective, and the other person is able to knock over whatever defenses you have. If you become overwhelmed, you may not have been allowed to experience a psychological apartness from your parent(s). When you tried to move apart, the parent(s) overcame your boundaries. Consequently, you may never have learned how to build boundaries strong enough to withstand assaults.

Admiration

An excessive need for admiration is another characteristic of underdeveloped narcissism. Others are expected to recognize how wonderful you are, and to let you know that they recognize your wonderfulness. The excessive aspect of this occurs when your need to be admired is an expectation you have of everyone, or almost everyone, and you are hurt, angry, and/or fearful when the sought-for admiration is not forthcoming.

You may be unaware of some of your admiration-seeking behaviors. Following are some attitudes and behaviors that indicate excessive seeking of admiration. Rate yourself on each item, using this scale: 1 – I never or almost never do this; 2 – I seldom do this; 3 – I sometimes do this; 4 – I do this often; 5 – I do this very frequently.

Admiration-Seeking Scale

1. I boast about my possessions.

2. I brag about my achievements, or my children, or whom I know.

3. I exaggerate, e.g., my accomplishments, salary, the cost of something I bought.

4. I go out of my way to do things for others, so they will feel indebted or grateful.

5. I use every opportunity to point out how much I do for others.

6. I take or seek unearned credit.

7. I make sure others know how much effort I expend on their behalf.

8. I try to associate with people I think have higher status than I do.

9. I sell myself at every opportunity.

10. I complain, whine, carp, and so forth, so that others will know how much I suffer, and admire my fortitude.

Add your ratings. If your total ratings are 40–50, you have considerable admiration-seeking behavior. If you score 30–39, you have many such behaviors; 20–29 you seek admiration for some things on some occasions; 10–19 you have few such behaviors; and 1–9 you have almost none of these behaviors.

Do you resort to extreme measures in your quest for admiration? Extreme measures are those such as these:

- Going into debt to buy unneeded things for others to notice

- Talking loudly and often about how great you and yours are

- Embellishing everything about yourself to be bigger, better, etc.

- Always putting your name on work you did not do or to which you contributed little

These are behaviors that can be destructive to your relationships and, in some cases, to your well-being.

Admiration can feel good when received unexpectedly and when voluntarily offered. Many people have others they admire for one reason or another, e.g., overcoming adversity, accomplishing something difficult. There is also a tendency to glamorize and admire "heroes"(both genders). It could be that part of admiration-seeking behavior is a desire to be a hero, or to be grander than others. Embedded in admiration-seeking behavior there seem to be attitudes similar to those of infants who consider themselves:

- wonderful
- grand
- omniscient
- marvelous
- omnipotent
- powerful

Infants look to others to mirror their self-perception of being admirable. Some behaviors are learned and reinforced because they produce the desired effect, i.e., being admired. For example, some people learn that when they sacrifice their well-being to take care of someone else, there are other people who will express admiration for their sacrifice.

Unique and Special

Each of us is unique. Even twins are not exactly the same in every respect. Our genetic makeup, environmental influences, and experiences interact to produce billions of different people. So, in certain respects, each of us *is* unique. However, there are more similarities than differences, and the need to be considered unique and special by almost everyone speaks to a deep human desire. How do you feel about the following:

- Being labeled or categorized?
- Someone making assumptions about what you believe based on one of your characteristics, e.g., race?
- Others judging you on your racial/ethnic designation, or other such identifiers?
- Someone being contemptuous or patronizing because of your "identification"?
- Being overlooked or ignored?

My hunch is that you do not like experiencing any of these, and you want to be perceived as an individual. That feeling is not unusual. The negative outcomes of the deep desire to be seen as unique and special are behaviors and attitudes such as the following:

- Wearing outrageous dress or behaving for shock value
- Ignoring rules and regulations
- Engaging in risky behavior
- Being insensitive to others' feelings and needs
- Wanting rewards without having to work for them

- Demanding that your needs take preference over those of others

- Flaunting your breaking of society's values and norms

- Expecting others to bend or break rules for you

Some of these examples have two sides: the personal statement and the desire to be recognized. For instance, outrageous dress or behaving for shock value has a personal component, i.e., you can dress as you wish. The recognition component speaks to your motive, i.e., shock value. If you are dressing to please yourself, it doesn't mean you are doing so out of a conscious desire to be considered unique and special. The extent to which you go to be seen as unique and special indicates how deep-seated this need is for you.

Grandiosity

Infants demonstrate age-appropriate grandiosity that is supposed to gradually become more realistic as the child grows and matures. In adults, arrogant and contemptuous attitudes displayed toward others are termed *grandiosity*, and this is not age-appropriate. There are a number of common phrases that capture some of this attitude, e.g.:

- nose stuck in the air

- thinks he/she is better than everyone else

- looks down on others

- doesn't know his/her limitations

- always knows what's best for everyone

- considers him/herself to be in charge or the ultimate authority

- cannot take "no" for an answer

- expects others to kowtow to him/her

Grandiosity is an extreme form of confidence. Confidence is desirable and acceptable, and considerable time and effort can be expended in becoming self-confident. Being cocky or arrogant is less desirable or acceptable. Both attitudes suggest a disdain for others as not being as great or important as you see yourself. Having an attitude of superiority doesn't go over well with others. In fact, arrogance and contemptuousness arouse fury in others.

We all know people we think fit this description. However, we are less likely to be aware of our own grandiosity, no matter how little of it we have. You may not be as grandiose, arrogant, or contemptuous as the person you envision, but you may still exhibit some of those characteristics. There is a line between confidence and arrogance, and, at times, that line may be hard to see or to describe.

Rate your responses to the following: 1 – I never feel this way; 2 – I seldom feel this way; 3 – I feel this way, but try to feel differently; 4 – I feel this way sometimes; 5 – I usually feel this way.

Awareness of Personal Grandiosity Scale

1. My ideas, opinions, etc. have more validity and importance than those of most other people.

2. When I see a homeless person, I wonder why he/she doesn't try to help him/herself more.

3. If others worked as hard as I do, or were as smart as I am, they could have what I have.

4. I should be respected, admired, and given preferential treatment for what I've accomplished.

5. I can work the system so that I come out on top.

6. I should not have to "pay the dues" that others do.

7. Whatever I do should be recognized as exceptional and vastly superior to what others do.

8. I know more or better than others do.

9. I'm better than others at almost everything.

10. Most people do not have anything of value that I need, want, or can use.

Scoring

Review the items you rated 3 or more. Listed below are some of the attitudes and behaviors that can be your focus for trying to tame your grandiosity. Let's take each item and see what modifications you could institute.

1. You can consciously remind yourself that you are not the authority or the "last word" on anything, much less on everything.

2. You can help those more unfortunate than you in many ways; e.g., volunteer; make charitable contributions; work to change community, state, and national policies. Having compassion for others helps you be the person you want to be.

3. Celebrate your good fortune, but realize not everyone had the resources or assistance you did. Maybe you did work harder, but you can feel good about what you have done or what you have without needing to "put down" others.

4. You do deserve respect, as does everyone. Be sure to both give and receive respect, and do not expect that it will be given to you automatically.

5. Explore your need to win at any cost. You may be paying an unintended price for winning because your competitiveness, ruthless behavior, and willingness to be unfair do have an impact on your relationships. It would be quite rare for this attitude to be present in only one part of your life, e.g., work. Unconsciously, you may be extending it to other parts of your life, where it has a negative impact.

6. You gain respect and admiration from almost everyone when you "pay your dues." By skipping ahead, you arouse negative feelings, and there is always the sneaking suspicion that you didn't have everything it takes; that you bribed your way or someone else did, and that you are lacking something essential.

7. Everything you do is not exceptional or vastly superior, although some things may be. Start recognizing the accomplishments of others, the adverse circumstances that some people have to overcome, the things you cannot do or cannot do well, and begin to appreciate what others can do, and give up having a superior attitude.

8. You may know more or better about some things, but this is not global, i.e., you do not know more about everything; nor do you know best about anything. Adopt the attitude that there is always more to know about anything, that others can and do know some things you do not, and that learning is a continual process. Become open to learning from everyone. Recognize that you are *not* the other person and cannot know what is better for him/her. You may have some experiences and ideas, but you are not the other person, and what seems right for you may not be right for him/her.

9. It doesn't hurt to be modest. You may be better at many things, but not everything: nor does your being better mean that the other person is inferior. His/her talents, abilities, and expertise lie in other areas. Plus, you still have something to learn from those who know less than you do.

10. Open yourself up to experiencing, and you will find that others do have something of value to offer you. That something can be knowledge, an attitude, a different perspective, understanding, an

awareness, inspiration, an original thought, etc. The possibilities are endless.

Entitlement

An entitlement attitude goes along with the desire to be considered unique and special. With an entitlement attitude, laws, rules, and/or expectations do not apply to you, they are merely suggestions for other people. You become very angry when you do not get your way, or what you want when you want it. Although the tantrums you had when you were two years old may have ceased overtly, internally they still exist, and are displayed covertly.

If you are confronted or caught breaking the rules, or revealed as breaking the law, your attitude might be "What's your point?" That rule, law, or whatever did not mean *you*. Some vestige of guilt might be attached, but your prevailing attitude would be one of outrage that anyone dared to say you were wrong or in error.

An entitlement attitude is displayed in a variety of ways, but the underlying assumption is that your expectation is that your needs are the most important in any interaction, and they *will* be met, regardless of cost or perceived unfairness. To show just how everyday events can reflect your entitlement attitude, rate yourself on the following items.

Use this scale: 1 – I almost never do or feel this; 2 – I seldom do or feel this; 3 – sometimes I do or feel this; 4 – I often do or feel this; 5 – I very often do or feel this.

Your Personal Feelings of Entitlement Scale

1. I fret about having to wait in line.

2. I will enter someone's space without knocking or asking permission. (Even entering your child's room counts here.)

3. I will interrupt someone who's talking.

4. I walk up to a couple or group and start talking, or I will change the subject.

5. I find ways around established rules and guidelines.

6. I think that, when people point out I am breaking rules or guidelines, that they are overreacting or being unfair.

7. I give orders or make demands with the expectation of being obeyed.

8. I go to meetings and sit at the end of the table (either the head or the foot).

9. I ask my boss or coworkers for numerous favors so I can do something I want to do, or to get out of work.

10. I call or visit others when I feel like it, without prior notice.

11. I use others' possessions without their permission (family members also count here).

12. I rummage through others' belongings or territory, e.g., medicine cabinet, husband's wallet, child's closet, coworker's desk.

13. I will take over and start running things my way.

14. I will tell someone how he/she should, ought, or must do something, or how to think or feel.

15. I get angry when I do not receive the recognition, deference, or preferential treatment I feel I deserve.

16. I touch others without first asking permission, e.g., hugs, pats.

17. I make unsolicited comments about someone's appearance, dress, hair, weight gain or loss, etc.

18. I play the radio, television, or stereo loudly, all the time, even when I am sharing space with others.

19. I change the radio station when I am riding in someone else's car.

20. I expect others to know what I want and give it to me.

Scoring

Add your ratings to derive a total score ranging between 20–100. If your score is 80–100, you can consider yourself as having numerous entitlement attitudes and behaviors. With a score between 60–79, you exhibit many such behaviors and attitudes. With a score of 40–50, you show some entitlement attitudes. And if your score is below 40 you have few such attitudes and behaviors. With scores above 40, you will want to increase your awareness of when you assume an attitude of entitlement.

The reason this entitlement behaviors and attitude scale is longer than the other scales is that there are so many unconscious behaviors that indicate an entitlement attitude. The ones listed here are only samples, and you can probably add others to this list. All you have to do is to think about your experience of others' behaviors that produced even mild discomfort for you.

Many entitlement attitudes are displayed by boundary violations and you will want to pay particular attention to your behaviors relative to these. Ask yourself how you might be unconsciously violating others' boundaries. Increasing your awareness of your behavior can reduce your unconscious violations of others' boundaries, and increase your awareness of when your own boundaries are being violated. Greater awareness of both states can lead to stronger, more resilient boundaries for you personally, and contribute to having better interpersonal relationships.

Envy

Envy is a waste of time and effort. When you are envious of someone's accomplishments, possessions, characteristics, or relationships, you feel that he/she received something you should have received because you are more worthy than he/she is. Furthermore, there may be resentment on your part because you also feel that the other person is inferior and does not deserve whatever it is that is arousing the envy.

What is also referred to here as envy is the desire to have others want what you have. When you feel envied, your attitude has a feeling of superiority embedded in it, as if you are saying that you must be better than the other person to have the envied thing. This desire speaks to a need to "lord it over others," to want to be seen as unique and special, and to have others admire you to the extent that their focus is on "You."

How much of your time is spent envying others? Do you feel that someone:

- Does not deserve his/her good fortune

- Is lucky

- Cut you out of something you should have received

- Was given something he/she did not warrant or deserve

- Was given preferential treatment you should have received

- Is admired and gets the attention that you want

- Has possessions you wish were yours

- Does not work as hard as you do, but seems to be better rewarded

- Has an ideal relationship you feel you should have

- Has accumulated goods and wealth you also want?

These examples of envious yearnings and desires give you some idea of just how widespread envy can be. Whether you envy someone, want others to envy you, or both, you are wasting your time and efforts. Your time would be better spent on doing what it takes to get what you want; to understand yourself better, your desires and your motives; and to make constructive use of the resources, abilities, and talents you do have. When you build your psychological self, you will not need the envy of others to feel good about yourself.

Power and Control

Infants feel omnipotent, i.e., they feel that they "cause" things to happen. Their discomfort is attended to and they do not recognize or understand that there is another person taking care of them. The infant feels all-powerful. As infants gradually become aware of other people and begin to understand their own individuality, their sense of power and control begins to become more realistic.

If the child has mature, nurturing parents, this gradual awareness also incorporates a growing awareness of him/herself as an individual. This defining and redefining of self-identity continues throughout life, as does an understanding of the possibilities and limits of personal power and control.

The other side of feeling powerful and in control is feeling helpless and powerless, where the person feels unable to be effective, or unable to prevent external and/or internal forces from having an impact on him/her. When someone is helpless, he or she can do nothing but stand there and take whatever life has to offer.

The following are some feelings, attitudes, and behaviors about your need for power and control. Rate yourself on each using:

1—Almost never; 2—Sometimes; 3—Often; 4—Very frequently; 5—Almost always.

Awareness of Your Need for Personal Power and Control Scale

1. I become upset when things do not go as I plan.

2. I expect others to do what I tell them to do.

3. I expect prompt compliance with my orders or demands.

4. I give lots of orders.

5. I plan revenge when thwarted.

6. I feel ineffective.

7. I look to others to rescue me.

8. I become hurt at the least hint of criticism.

9. I am easily overwhelmed by tasks, demands, etc.

10. I obey others' commands and orders, but I feel resentful.

Scoring

The scoring for this scale is different than in previous scales. Add your ratings for the first five items. This is your Power score. It will range from 5–25 with 18–25 indicating high power needs, 11–17 indicating moderate power needs, and 10 or below indicating slight power needs. Add your ratings for items 6–10. This is your Helpless score. Scores will range from 5–25. Use the same ranges and designations, e.g., high, as those used for the Power score.

These items have only a few of the many possible behaviors and attitudes that suggest power or helplessness as a characteristic. If you scored 18+ on Power needs you will want to better understand the following:

● Why is it so important for you to control others?

● Why do you consciously or unconsciously consider others as extensions of yourself, and thus under your control?

● What impact do these behaviors and attitudes have on your relationships?

If your Helplessness scores are 18+ you are displaying attitudes and behaviors that convey the following:

● A desire to be rescued

● A lack of independence

● A yearning for nurturance

● Low or absent self-confidence

● Low self-efficacy

● A need for boundary development

● A willingness to let others take the lead

● Acquiescence to others' manipulation and control

● A conviction that others know better than you do

● A compliant attitude

These are the attitudes and behaviors that leave you open to "catching" others' emotions, and a tendency to be manipulated by others. These would have a high priority for making some changes.

Strategies

Some strategies for building your psychological "self" are presented throughout this chapter to address specific attitudes or behaviors.

Following are the general strategies for all topics and a suggested process to follow for changing the behaviors and attitudes you decide to change.

Before initiating changes you need to do the following:

1. Become more aware of your personal behavior.

2. Accept that there are aspects of yourself that you cannot see.

3. Listen to the comments of those people whom you trust.

The discussion and scales in this chapter are the foundation for your becoming more aware of possible underdeveloped narcissism. There is enough specificity about the various attitudes and behaviors to guide you in your self-assessment. Accept that you are very likely to have some areas of underdeveloped narcissism and that you *cannot see* these aspects of yourself. You have to tentatively accept that there is some part of you that still needs to be developed.

One way to increase your awareness is to carefully listen to what others tell you about your behavior and/or attitude. You do not have to agree with what they say, but if the people you ask can be trusted, you can gain some valuable information about parts of yourself that you cannot see. Stay open to the possibility that you do have some aspects of self that could be better developed.

The basic steps to create change are simple. You will need a notebook and a writing instrument.

1. Select a behavior and/or attitude you want to change.

2. Write a short statement in the notebook about what you are proposing to change.

3. List three to five things you can do to change. For example, your entries might look something like this:

   ● I need to become more aware of my entitlement behavior and attitudes.

   ● When I have to wait in line, remind myself that it's not personal; others also have things to do, and they are also impatient.

   ● I need to find some way to amuse myself while I have to wait; for example, meditate, plan the sequence for my errands, think of what I want for a birthday party, watch others around me and try to guess something about them, and so forth.

4. Keep a weekly diary in the notebook of your progress toward your objective(s). Try to record each event, what you felt, how you implemented your strategy, and how you felt afterwards. This can be brief,

but it is important that you have a record, so that you can see your progress even though it can be slight.

5. Be patient with yourself. You did not arrive at the person you are today in a week, month, or year. It took time to develop you as you currently are, and it takes time to make changes.

6. Set a time frame for evaluating your progress, such as weekly, monthly, or after six weeks. Read your diary and reflect on what changes you can see.

7. When you feel you are well on your way to making the desired changes, start the process of change for another set of attitudes and behaviors.

Material presented in this chapter emphasized building your psychological "self" through underdeveloped narcissism, and that is a continuing thread in the remaining chapters. There are other aspects of narcissism to be explored on the way to promoting your healthy adult narcissism. The next chapter focuses on emotions and developing appropriate empathy.

Chapter 7

Emotional Strength

Some people feel that their emotions are leading them astray, e.g., having too much empathy, and this notion is a major premise of this book. You may wonder why so much attention is given to building your emotional "self." After all, you can readily access your feelings, or have them triggered by others. This chapter will show you how to retain ready access to your emotions, while you reduce or eliminate your susceptibility to having your emotions triggered by others. It is hoped that you will get ideas and instructions to help you block others' unwanted access to your feelings, whether that access is due to internal or external forces. The intent is to be more in charge of who, what, and when others have access to your feelings.

You Can Change Your Feelings

Ellis (1973) in his Rational-Emotive Theory proposes that the specific event does not cause the reaction or response. He believes that the feelings about the event cause the reaction. Following are three possible reactions to an event. Each shows how the chosen feeling leads to a different response.

Suppose your mother tells you that you need a haircut. When she says that, you start to feel that you are failing to live up to her standards, which in turn, arouses guilt. Your response is to tell her you that you are an adult and can make such decisions for yourself. Or, instead of becoming defensive, you feel that your mother is just trying to be helpful. You feel affection for her efforts, thank her for noticing, and tell her that you will be sure to get a haircut soon. Still another response would be based on your realization that your mother has no way of knowing that you are letting your hair grow for a new hairstyle. In this instance, you are amused at her comment and tell her why you are letting your hair grow. Thus, the same event can produce three different feelings with three different possible responses. This is what Ellis means by saying that the *feeling* causes the reaction, not the event itself.

This theory goes on to suggest that we cause or choose our emotions, and that many of them are based on "irrational beliefs." An *irrational belief* is one that does not have a basis in objective reality, is illogical, and contributes to self-defeating behaviors. For example, an irrational belief is believing that you must be perfect. The perfectionist, in his/her quest for perfection, is never able to be pleased or satisfied with anyone or anything. The need for perfection is the driving force that causes the perfectionist, and those in relationship with him or her, to be miserable and always on edge trying to achieve the impossible, i.e., perfection. Wanting to be good, to get or do something right or better, is desirable. Having to be perfect or to achieve perfection is not desirable.

Two concepts are used throughout this discussion to help you better understand some of your reactions. They are (1) we choose our emotions, and (2) some emotions are experienced on the basis of irrational beliefs. Some irrational beliefs are similar to previously discussed faulty assumptions. We will continue to work on how your feelings are triggered, and how your feelings can be expressed appropriately, modified, or even changed.

Why Focus on Emotions?

Why give so much attention to emotions? There are several reasons why taking an in-depth look at emotions is helpful. These reasons are as follow:

- emotions affect physical health

- emotions affect interpersonal relationships

- emotions affect our self-esteem

Furthermore, the basic premise of this book is that currently you are being caught and enmeshed or overwhelmed by others' emotions, and you want to change this. To help you develop better emotional shielding, it is first necessary to build up your emotional self.

The evidence continues to mount that the effects of emotions have an impact on physical health. For example, anger and hostility play a significant role in heart disease, high blood pressure, and various gastrointestinal conditions. Happiness provides a boost to the immune system that helps to ward off infections, hope and optimism have significant impacts on recovery from surgery and disease, and the cumulative effects of continuing emotional distress make themselves felt in all parts of the body. How you feel about yourself, your ability to control and influence what happens to you, and your satisfaction with your life and your relationships can all have effects on your physical health.

Relationships are important, as these are the support systems that provide you with connections to others. The quality of your relationships is reflected in the feelings you have, such as those experienced as isolation and alienation. Such feelings are common when relationships are absent or unsatisfactory. On the other hand, when your relationships are satisfactory, you are more likely to have more positive feelings of being connected to others and to the world.

Another important component in relationships is how you feel about yourself, because these feelings can be projected onto others easily. What happens in this instance is different from what happens in transference. *Transference* occurs when the perceived similarities and reactions of someone you knew in a past relationship are unconsciously assigned to someone you know in a current relationship. *Projection* occurs when you take a part of yourself, such as an unwanted feeling like anger, assign that part to another person, and then react to that person as if he/she actually had the projected characteristic. Emotions and relationships are very complex, but it can be helpful to understand your emotions and see how they affect your relationships.

Your emotions also affect your self-esteem in many ways. For example, if you feel you have been betrayed, you may perceive yourself as foolish or stupid for not having seen through the falseness of that person. For another example of how your emotions affect your self-esteem, consider how much more easily you can forgive yourself for making mistakes when you are pleased with your overall achievements. It's difficult to feel good about yourself if you are feeling any of the following emotions:

- down in the dumps
- out of sorts
- have an attitude
- irritable
- on edge
- suspicious that others are out to "get you"
- fearful about the future
- bogged down in uncertainty and ambiguity

You cannot feel particularly effective, competent, or self-assured when you are experiencing any of these conditions, and you may doubt your self-efficacy. All of this can significantly affect your self-esteem.

A Vocabulary for Feelings

There are many words to describe or label feelings, but most people use only a few, and many of the words used are ambiguous. That is, the listener cannot be sure what that person's meaning or feeling is from the words that are used to describe it. Developing a broader and more descriptive vocabulary to describe what you feel can sharpen your awareness of what you are feeling, allow you to be more immediate when expressing your feelings, and make all of your communications clearer.

Your vocabulary for feelings can be developed by:

● Learning more descriptive words to describe what you feel

● Describing the sensations aroused within yourself.

● Using metaphors.

● Building or creating word pictures.

Here are four exercises to get you started on building your vocabulary to describe your feelings.

Exercise 7.1: Descriptive Words

Materials: Five sheets of unlined paper; felt markers, crayons, or oil pastels; a writing instrument; a dictionary

Procedure: At the top of each sheet of paper write one of the following words: *Safe, Affectionate, Disgruntled, Charmed,* and *Threatening.*

Take each word, one at a time, and complete the following instructions.

1. Look up the definition for the word in the dictionary.

2. As you read the definitions and the synonyms, pay attention to the images that are aroused for you, e.g., a color or colors, person(s), situation(s), feeling(s), and so forth.

3. Draw and/or color all of the images that were aroused.

4. Give each drawing or coloring a title. Remember, you should have five pages, one for each word, so you will have five products and five titles.

5. If an image does not arise from your reading of the dictionary meaning, try to visualize an image that seems to capture the essence of the defined word for you. Use that for your drawing or coloring.

Exercise 7.2: Sensations

Materials: Two sheets of paper and a writing instrument

Procedure: Sit in silence and read the following scenes one at a time. Complete the exercise for one scene before moving on to the next one.

1. As you read the scene, imagine that you are present either as a participant or an observer.

2. Become aware of your body and what it is feeling; no matter how mild or slight the feeling, e.g., heart racing, palms sweating, head aching, feet jiggling. Pay attention to your entire body.

3. Write down all the bodily sensations you experience.

Some of the sensations you feel you bring with you to the exercise, some are the result of your doing the exercise, and some are aroused as you place yourself in the scene.

Scene 1: You are falling asleep and you hear an unfamiliar sound.

Scene 2: Someone does or says something unexpectedly that arouses a very intense feeling.

Exercise 7.3: Metaphors

Materials: Three sheets of paper; felt markers, crayons, or oil pastels

Procedure: Draw or create a splash of colors for the images and feelings that are aroused as you visualize each of the following metaphors.

"As jittery as a long-tailed cat in a room full of rocking chairs."

"Falling as flower petals on a lily pad in a pond of water."

"I'm on cloud nine."

Use different colors for each feeling and/or image in each metaphor.

Exercise 7-4: Word Pictures

Materials: Tape recorder and tape, scene from a magazine, or a personal photograph

Procedure: Record a description of the scene or photograph. Make your description as much like a story as you can.

1. Describe the background, colors, scents, and sounds.

2. Describe the people involved in terms of their age, gender, work or education, and relationships with each other.

3. Describe clothes, hairstyles, jewelry, etc.

4. Give a running account of what is happening in the scene.

5. Describe what the participants are feeling.

6. Describe what you imagine will happen to the people in your story in the future.

When you are finished recording your word picture, rewind the tape and listen to it. Let yourself become aware of any omissions, scanty descriptions, or places where you could be clearer. Pay particular attention to your descriptions of feelings.

Mild Versions of Emotions

If you are emotionally susceptible, that may mean you are not aware of experiencing mild versions of some emotions. You may become aware of these feelings only when they become intense. Senders tend to have intense emotions and to be able to project them. "Catchers" are open to receiving these projections, but they may overlook or ignore warning signs of possible projections and identifications because the warning signs they feel are mild. When you pay attention to what you are feeling in the moment, you can do the following:

● Better understand what you perceive to be happening.

● Tune in to what you are experiencing that is yours alone, and is not a projection.

● Screen out projections from others.

● Increase your awareness of the milder emotions that may be masked by more intense feelings.

● Become aware of your resistance and defenses.

● Begin to analyze your response(s).

● Understand when you need to employ your emotional shielding.

These are all benefits and they can aid you in reducing or eliminating your susceptibility to "catching" others' feelings. But first, you need to increase your attention and awareness of the milder versions of some emotions. In the following set of exercises, each one offers a variety of ways to respond. They are intended to make you more aware of some of the milder experiences of basic feelings, e.g., fear. Try to complete all the exercises, and try to work in a variety of forms, e.g., make a drawing and construct a collage, write a poem and an essay.

These exercises can give you ideas for increasing your awareness that will suit your personality. They can be completed by doing a drawing, constructing a collage, writing an essay, creating a poem, or visualizing a scene and drawing it. Each medium, the necessary materials, and the basic procedures are briefly described. We begin with a brief introduction for each form, or medium, that will be used in the exercises.

Drawing

Drawings can be realistic, symbolic, or abstract. They can be anything you want them to be. For example, you could draw a scene from your life that illustrates the designated topic, or a fantasized scene, or a splash of colors, shapes, or symbols. You can draw cartoons or stick figures. You can do scribble drawings or detailed illustrations.

The materials you need are felt markers, crayons, or oil pastels; large sheets of newsprint paper; pen or pencil. If you intend to use drawing as your primary medium, consider purchasing a pad of newsprint 18 x 24-inches (or larger) from a craft store. This way, you can draw on the pad and have a "book" of your products.

The procedure is to find a place with a table or other flat surface for drawing that is also free from intrusions and distractions. Draw whatever emerges for you.

Collages

A collage is a combination of numerous cut-out pictures, colors and/or shapes, glued onto a page to depict a concept, feeling, or characteristic in pictorial symbols. The intent is to illustrate the many facets of some feeling or other abstraction in symbolic form.

The materials needed are: solid color memory book paper; a collection of magazines and catalogs from which to cut out pictures that will symbolize the topic of the collage; scissors; glue stick or paste; felt markers, crayons, or oil pastels.

The procedure is to cut out pictures from your magazines or catalogs that symbolize the topic of the collage, arrange them, and then glue them onto the paper. You may want to outline the pictures in a shape that captures the essence of the topic for you. Use the markers, crayons, or oil pastels to draw symbols and shapes for any items you wanted to include in the collage but for which you were unable to find pictures.

Essays

These can be any length, from a paragraph to several pages. Your essays should include the following:

- a description of the designated topic

- how you experience it; i.e., what it feels like to you

- situations or events in your life that reflect or illustrate the topic

- any other thoughts and/or feelings you want to include

The materials needed are paper or a notebook, and a writing instrument. If you prefer to use a computer to write your essay, you may do so.

The procedure is to sit in a quiet place free from distractions and interruptions. Begin by writing the topic at the top of the page and compose your essay around that topic. As you will not be graded on technical quality, e.g., grammar and punctuation, you can just let your essay emerge. If you find it helpful, develop an outline before beginning your essay. I find it helpful to list the points I want to be sure to include, but not to write a formal outline.

Poems

There are times when thoughts, ideas, images, and feelings can be expressed in phrases and words, but not in complete sentences. Poems can be a way of expressing these, without having to develop sentences such as those used in an essay. It can be very interesting to try to write a poem. There are many types of poems, and they do not have to rhyme.

The materials needed are paper and a writing instrument, or you may want to create your poem on the computer.

The procedure is to sit quietly and reflect on the topic or concept about which you will write a poem. Allow images and impressions to emerge, but do not try to edit or change them. Write all the things that pop into your mind and that you feel or sense. After you finish, read the list, and organize your different words or lines, or part of them, into a poem.

Visualizing

This technique also uses the medium of drawing. The intent is to use your creative side to enhance and expand your experiences, and not to rely just on thoughts or cognitive processes for understanding.

The materials needed are the same as those for drawing. The procedure is to sit in silence, close your eyes if you wish, and allow images, feelings, and impressions about the topic to emerge. You may see a scene from your past, people you know or knew, colors, and so forth. When you are ready, open your eyes and draw what emerged for you.

The Emotions

Five basic emotions; guilt, shame, fear, sadness, and happiness are the focus for the next set of exercises. Each will be briefly discussed in terms of its impact on your emotional "self" and its influence on your behavior. Some milder versions of each emotion are also discussed. The exercises are intended to expand your awareness of the milder versions. Awareness means to be able to sense and describe what that emotion is like for you in terms of your sensations, thoughts, and actions. Most of the emotions discussed are not pleasant, and you will want to consider how you may avoid experiencing even the milder versions of these emotions. Once you have increased your awareness, you can then take steps to:

- Analyze the feeling

- Judge the validity of the feeling in terms of how rational it is

- Understand how your faulty assumptions help to trigger the feeling

- Use your cognitive resources to prevent yourself from becoming mired in the feeling

In addition, your analyses will help you to better judge when the emotion was "caught" from someone else, and this, in turn, can lead you to more effective use of your emotional shielding. The feelings discussed are: guilt, shame, fear, sadness, and happiness.

Guilt

Guilt is aroused when you perceive that you have failed to live up to what you consider to be your moral and ethical standards. You feel that you have done "wrong" in some way. For example, you acted in a way that is contrary to your standards, or you failed to do something, and that failure was contrary to your standards.

Guilt is an outcome of the acculturation of family, community, and societal standards. We incorporate and internalize the standards of those people in our world, and when we are caught acting contrary to those standards, we learn that we have not met others' expectations. For example, incurring the displeasure or disappointment of parents teaches us the experience of feeling guilt.

We also learn that there is usually a way to make up or atone for failure to meet the standards of those in our world, unlike the case for shame where there is no atoning. (See the section "Shame" below.) An act of atonement is done to rectify the omission or act that failed to meet expectations. That is, you can apologize for what was done or not done, or pay a penalty. Although there are some acts for which there can never be adequate atonement, there are many for which some form of atonement or payment can be made.

Milder versions of guilt include the following: feeling blameworthy, remorseful, delinquent, culpable, and/or regretful.

Exercise 7.5: Feeling Guilty

Directions: Choose a medium and create something that expresses how guilt feels to you. You may choose to draw, make a collage, write an essay or poem, or you may visualize something and then draw it.

Shame

Shame is the feeling that you:

● are inadequate

● do not measure up to standards or expectations

● are not as good, smart, etc., as others

● have something "wrong" with you

● are fatally flawed

● can never "get it right"

● are not "good enough"

This feeling is one that speaks about the very core of your being, i.e., you are found "wanting" in some essential respect. As mentioned above, shame, unlike guilt, does not have any mechanism for atonement or remediation. The flaw to the "self" is permanent and cannot be "fixed," nor is there a way to compensate for the flaw. It then becomes important to the individual to hide or mask the flaw, so that others do not perceive how unworthy he/she is. A considerable amount of time and effort may go into hiding shame.

Shame is also experienced as:

● becoming self-conscious

● being ill at ease

● embarrassment

● feeling disgraced

● feeling that you or something about you is not acceptable

You most likely have experienced one or more of these milder versions of shame, but probably did not recognize it, or call it shame. These are common feelings experienced by almost everyone. You even may have tried to mask or hide the ill-at-ease feeling that you had, or deny to yourself that you felt that way.

Much time and effort is spent in covering up shame and its milder versions; time and effort that could be used more constructively. As you work through the exercises to build your psychological, emotional, creative, and inspirational "self," you will find that you gain a greater acceptance of yourself—flaws and all. You will also find that you are some or all of the following:

● adequate in many ways

● worthy

● good enough

- meeting your own standards and expectations sufficiently well

- reducing your experience of shame and its milder versions

This self-acceptance and willingness to work on "self" provides you with valuable tools for building your emotional shielding.

Exercise 7.6: Shame

Directions: Select a medium and create something that depicts two or more milder versions of shame, e.g., feeling embarrassed, and what shame feels like to you.

Fear

Fear is a basic emotion experienced from birth. This is in contrast to guilt and shame that appear to be learned. With fear, the self is perceived to be in danger of being hurt or destroyed, and the body prepares to fight or flee. As you grow older, you may also fear the unknown, such as the future, new or different people, and other such changes. Your experiences can cause you to fear anything that has features associated with previous experiences where you were afraid, hurt, or psychologically damaged in some way. Fear is the body and mind's way of preparing you to defend yourself from real or fantasized danger.

Strengthening your boundaries and emotional shielding requires you to become more aware of when you experience milder versions of fear. Notice that the term "experience" is in the present tense. This is crucial for you to prevent and eliminate "catching" others' emotions. You must learn to pay more attention to when you are feeling:

- a sense of disquiet

- apprehensive

- alarm

- dread

You do not want to wait until you are in the throes of terror, horror, or panic before becoming aware that you are in danger. That can be, and often is, too late.

Exercise 7.7: Fear

Directions: Select a medium and create something that describes or illustrates each of the following milder emotional states: disquiet, apprehension, alarm, and dread. You should have four creations, each one illustrating one of these emotional states. When you finish, review your creations and construct a "feeling" abstract picture using different shades of one color for each of these four feelings. For example, if you selected red as the color, *disquiet* could be a pale pink, *apprehension* a deep or hot pink, *alarm* an orange-red, and *dread* a bright red. You may use any color you desire.

Sadness

Sadness is the feeling of loss of meaning, vitality, purpose, love, connections, and so forth, in your life. Such meanings may be tied to a person, a function, or other parts of your life. Something you want, consider to be valuable, or is essential to your well-being is missing, and you feel the emptiness it, or they, left behind.

A sad person can make you feel you should or ought to do something to help him/her to be more positive and cheerful. Your openness to feeling the other person's sadness can make you susceptible, and you begin to want to do anything so that the person will not be sad. What is really happening is that you are trying to keep *yourself* from feeling sad by cheering up the other person whose feeling of sadness you "caught." You do not want to feel sad, but the other person's sadness has captured you; and you are made to feel that the only way you can feel better is to help him/her feel better.

Understanding when you are feeling one of the milder versions of sadness can alert you to the possibility that you are in the position of "catching" the sender's feelings during an interaction with him/her. Becoming aware of milder feelings can give you an opportunity to withdraw and/or to employ your emotional shielding before it is too late and you are drawn to the other person's feelings. Feeling any of the milder versions of sadness listed below also can serve as notice to you that you are on your way to a downward spiral of depression when you are alone and experience a milder version of sadness. Intervening early can be effective in either instance.

Some of the milder versions of sadness are: dejection, unhappiness, gloom, melancholy, and feeling miserable; although, to be fair, feeling miserable can be somewhat intense. There are also words and phrases that describe milder versions of sadness, such as "feeling down" and "getting the blues."

Exercise 7.8: Sadness

Directions: Select a medium and illustrate or describe what sadness and its milder versions feel like to you. This exercise provides you with an opportunity to use symbols for the feeling, e.g., tears for sadness.

Happiness

At last, we now focus on a positive emotion. There is only one positive emotion in this discussion because you are not likely to "catch" positive emotions, nor are you likely to be troubled by them. It's the uncomfortable emotions that capture you and allow you to be manipulated by others. However, because you can also "catch" positive emotions such as happiness, it is discussed.

Being happy is a peak experience. It's more intense than pleasure, but less intense than joy. Happiness is also highly individualistic, because what triggers happy feelings for one person will not necessarily do that for another person. The same can be said for different periods in your life. For example, some things that caused you to be happy when you were a teenager do not make you happy today.

Focusing on happy feelings and their milder versions can be helpful to increase your awareness of personal well-being, and to identify activities, ways, and techniques to enhance and increase your happy feelings. Becoming more aware of the state of your well-being involves the following:

- Focusing more intently on the positives in your life

- Appraising more realistically the negatives and not-so-positives in your life

- Decreased whining, complaining, and carping

- Better physical health

- A boost to your immune system

- Realizing the meaning and purpose of your life

- Gaining a clearer perspective of your alternatives, choices, and decisions

- Understanding what actions you need to take

Moving toward the positive, i.e., toward happiness, without minimizing the negative, e.g., sadness, can do wonders for your well-being and relationships, and it is a goal that can be accomplished. You can work to achieve a focus on the positives that will produce happiness for you by becoming aware of increasing and enhancing your experiences of milder versions of happiness, such as: gladness, satisfaction, feeling carefree, pleasure, and/or cheerful. You will learn to recognize these moments, treasure them, and expand them. Your pain and misery will not be eliminated, just reduced to more manageable proportions. You will gain the feeling of more balance in your life, and create greater hope and optimism.

Exercise 7.9: Happy Moments

Directions: Make a list of those little things that produce a feeling of pleasure for you, those things that make you feel warm, allow you to smile, and so forth. They could be such things as watching a child play with a puppy or kitten; seeing egrets standing in a pond; reading something that makes you laugh out loud; trying on a garment in a new color, and liking what you see; hearing a favorite tune you haven't heard in a while; watching dolphins play in the ocean; seeing the first flowers of spring, or the first light snow of winter; Christmas lights, and so forth. There are many such moments in your life, and this list can serve as a reminder.

Exercise 7.10: Happy

Directions: Select two or more mediums and make some creations that illustrate or describe happiness and its milder versions. If you choose the medium of collage, you may want to copy some photographs to use, in addition to the list of materials provided earlier. Another variation would be to create a color wheel using shades of colors to illustrate the gradations of feelings for happiness, or the different categories of whatever causes you to feel milder feelings of happiness.

Chapter 8

Your Creative Self

Creativity is a characteristic of healthy adult narcissism and is something that can be achieved by everyone. You may have the mistaken idea that creativity can be attained only by people who have artistic or other talents. Talent usually is considered to be exceptional ability in a specialized area, e.g., art, music, dance, sports, science, and so forth. Talent, although it needs to be developed, is also generally thought of as something you are born with that cannot be acquired through training or education. It is believed that the talented person is just able to do whatever it is, easily and better than others. Training and education allow the talented person to excel, but the basis for this excellence is inborn.

This idea that creativity demands talent available only to those who are born with a special ability is nonsense. Everyone can be creative. You have the ability to be creative in some aspect of your life, and creativity does not require you to have specialized abilities. Creativity involves the following characteristics:

- invention

- originality

- novelty

- a different perspective, technique, or process

- a sense of wonder

- the production of something new

The new thing that is produced can be an idea, a means or method, a new way of looking at something, combining ingredients, tackling a problem, painting a picture, composing a musical score, or interpreting a role in a play. The possibilities for being creative are endless.

Exercise 8.1: Everyday Things

Materials: A sheet of paper and a writing instrument

Directions: This exercise can be done anywhere. It's best if you can be undisturbed, but that's not a requirement. Wherever you are, look around and list the things you see that someone had to create by first thinking up the original process for making it, then design, or indeed, craft it. For example, as I write this I'm sitting in my family room at home. When I look around I see many things designed and created by others. If I made a list, my list would show the following items—all of which involved original and creative thoughts by someone:

- paper clip
- remote control
- plastic
- vinyl inflatable toys
- craft kits
- television set
- air cleaner
- puzzle toys in trays for toddlers
- magazines on a variety of subjects
- professional journal with original research
- unbreakable eyeglass lens

And I haven't even mentioned the original art work in the room. Try to increase your awareness of the everyday things in your world that someone had to think of, create, and produce for the first time.

Now, let's turn to consideration of building your creativity. If you have completed some of the exercises in the previous chapters, you've begun to build your creativity by trying new or different ways to express your feelings and thoughts. Try to think of creativity as:

- An expression of the human condition
- A means for expressing that which cannot be adequately expressed in words
- The process of doing everyday things in a new or different way
- A realization that there is a better way to accomplish something
- How you can change your perspective
- An opening of your mind to new and different possibilities
- A development of a sense of wonder

● The means to refine a process to make it better, more functional, take fewer steps, or use fewer parts, etc.

● A way you can express your joy, misery, and everything in between

Expand your awareness of your world, your life, your "self." Become willing to try new ways of perceiving and doing.

Personal Characteristics and Creativity Scale

Rate yourself on each of the following; use the scale: 1—Very little or not at all; 2—A little; 3—Somewhat; 4—More than the average person; 5—Very much.

1.	Insightful	5 4 3 2 1
2.	Curious	5 4 3 2 1
3.	Imaginative	5 4 3 2 1
4.	Resourceful	5 4 3 2 1
5.	Reflective	5 4 3 2 1
6.	Informal	5 4 3 2 1
7.	Spontaneous	5 4 3 2 1
8.	Unconventional	5 4 3 2 1
9.	Wide interests	5 4 3 2 1
10.	Individualistic	5 4 3 2 1
11.	Adventurous	5 4 3 2 1
12.	Dreamy	5 4 3 2 1
13.	Flexible	5 4 3 2 1
14.	Open minded	5 4 3 2 1
15.	Dislike routine	5 4 3 2 1

Scoring

Add your ratings to derive a total score.

60–75: You have numerous characteristics associated with creative personalities.

45–59: You have more than an average number of characteristics associated with creative personalities.

30–44: You have some characteristics associated with creative personalities.

15–29: You tend to have characteristics that are associated with conventional personalities who are not generally identified as creative.

0–14: You have personality characteristics that are the opposite of those associated with creative personalities.

If you scored 30+, you probably will have little difficulty enhancing your creativity. If you scored below 30, you will have to work harder and become more conscious of what you can do to enhance your creativity. Either way, you can develop your creativity.

Enhancing Your Creativity

There are several behaviors and attitudes that you can adopt or change that will enhance your creativity. Now that you are focused on the topic, you can begin to think of ways that you can be more creative. What follows here are some suggestions to try that are intended to give you a needed push to work on your creativity. The behaviors and attitudes that will be helpful are as follow:

- encouraging your imagination
- paying attention to your dreams
- being open minded
- trying new perspectives
- breaking routines and habits
- allowing yourself to be silly
- being flexible
- encouraging divergent thinking
- practicing innovative thinking

Imagination

Two definitions for imagination in Webster's dictionary are "the power of the mind to form a mental image or concept of something that is unreal or not present," and "such power of the mind used creatively." These definitions describe imagination as an ability available to everyone. When you imagine something, you can form a mental image or a concept of something that is real but not present, or of something that is not real. The image could be a fantasy. The formation of images and/or concepts is the beginning of creative thought.

Have you ever heard the experssions "flight of imagination" or "figment of your imagination"? A flight of your imagination allows your thoughts to roam where they will, without you trying to control or manage them in a conscious way. The end of a flight of imagination often results in an outcome of thinking of something new; or you find yourself thinking about something old in an entirely different way.

Figments of your imagination are fantasized things that may or may not be present in reality. The important point here is this: when you give your imagination the freedom to go where it will and to wander freely, you will develop new and different perspectives.

Dreaming

Imagination and dreams are similar. Dreams can occur during sleep or while you are awake, e.g., daydreams. Either way, you are allowing your mind to access material from your unconscious, and the unconscious is a rich source for creativity. Although imagination usually works with real objects or people, in ways that are easily understood by your conscious mind, dreams appear in symbolic forms that need interpretation to be understood. To give you an idea of how this works, complete the following exercise.

Exercise 8.2: A Dream

Materials: One or more sheets of paper and a writing instrument

Directions: Sit in silence and recall a dream. It could be a dream you had the night before, a dream you had a long time ago, or a recurring dream. It's your dream. If you can recall only a fragment of the dream, use that. If all you have are some memories of feelings you experienced during the dream, use those.

Write your dream in the present tense, as if you are experiencing it while you write. Describe the dream in as much detail as you can, noting the characters, sounds, smells, your feelings, and the actions in the dream.

Once you have recorded your dream or dream fragment, read over what you wrote. Underline the words or phrases that seem most important to you as you are reading the dream. Do not underline entire sentences, just words and phrases.

The next step is to make a list of the words and phrases from your dream. These words and phrases are the symbols in your dream. These symbols have personal meaning for you, and relate to you and your life as it is, or as it was. Try to come up with eight to ten words and phrases. Beside each word or phrase, write a personal association, something that is about you. For example, you could have the following words and associations:

Words	Associations
birds	independence, freedom
flying	freedom from constraints
ocean	uncontrollable emotions

The words and their associations are yours; they are not predetermined ones. You select the symbols, i.e., the words, and you make the associations that are relevant for you. You may get stuck and be unable to think of an association. That's only to be expected. For the time being, let it go and return to it later.

The last step in this exercise is to use your associations to write a summary paragraph or page about yourself and your life as perceived through your dream symbols. When you finish this, you have interpreted your dream.

This exercise demonstrates how you can use the symbols that appear in either your waking or sleeping dreams to extend your creativity, because dreams frequently suggest new directions, perspectives, and so forth.

Open-mindedness

An openness to new ideas, new information, new perspectives, and new ways of being and doing can enhance your creativity. Become less quick to reject something just because it is new, different, or unknown. This does not mean you must accept everything that comes along, as that would be counterproductive. It does mean that you should be willing to give something that is new or different your careful consideration, before you accept or reject it. Whatever it is, it should not be automatically rejected just because it is new or different.

By remaining open to divergent ideas, you can begin learning how to accept aspects or parts of the new idea or event and figure out how you can incorporate it in a more creative way. You become less limited in what you can consider and produce, and that characteristic enhances your opportunities to be creative in many other ways.

New Perspectives

Adopting an attitude that you will seek out new perspectives is aligned with openness. If you have a mind-set that your perspective is the only "right" or best one, you will rule out other ways of perceiving. It is possible that your perspective is the "right" or "best" one, but you cannot be certain of that until you have carefully considered other perspectives.

Additionally, considering other perspectives can enrich your own. For example, there is the story about the little boy who was given the task of drawing something, but he could not think of anything to draw, so he left the page blank. His teacher looked at the blank page and commented that he had produced a fine field of snow. The teacher was not only kind, she gave the child another perspective for looking at what was on the page. The boy was happy with the new perspective because he had been feeling like a failure for not being able to think of anything to draw, and the teacher was able to see something positive.

You do not have to consult other people to get additional perspectives, although that can be helpful. Your openness and willingness to consider other perspectives will allow you to think of various ways of seeing, doing, or perceiving. To be creative requires you to be able to generate additional perspectives.

Breaking Routines and Habits

It's easy to get into a rut where you think and act without conscious consideration of what you are doing. Take a look at the various daily routines and habits you currently have. For example, consider your morning routine of getting up and ready for the day. Do you perform certain acts in the same order every day? Do you feel irritated or out of sorts when you have to change your routine? I know that I get really irritated when the morning newspaper fails to arrive, or is incomplete. It's a part of my morning routine to read the paper and when it is not available I miss it. The funny thing is it doesn't bother me to not read the morning paper when I am out of town, even when a paper is readily available.

The primary point here is that it is an excellent idea for you to evaluate some of your habits and routines. Once you have some idea of how many routines you have, you can try doing the same thing in a different way. For example, you could do some of the following:

● Drive another route to work or school

● Turn the car radio off, and drive in silence

● Go for a short walk in the evening instead of sitting at home watching TV

● Change the seating arrangement at your family dinner table

● Wash your hair first (or last) when you shower

● Clean house on a day other than your usual day

There are many such routines that can be altered. The result of breaking a routine can be that you become more alert and aware of what you are doing. Acts become mindful and intentional, and you enhance your awareness of what you are observing, feeling, and doing. You can then begin to consider other alternatives, access new ideas, and see new possibilities. You actually can see things for the first time that were always there to be seen, but were previously overlooked or ignored, because they were the background for your routine.

The same can be said for some of your habits. Some habits are beneficial and can be retained. However, examining your habits may reveal that some are being performed in a mindless manner and without conscious intention. There may be some of those that can be modified. Bringing greater awareness to what you do can only enhance your creativity.

Being Silly

Do you feel foolish when you do silly things? Silly as in nonsensical, funny, and without any purpose except to laugh. Look at children and how they play. They do things for fun and have a good time doing it. They do not worry about:

- doing it right
- staying inside the lines
- playing by someone's rules
- others laughing at them
- making mistakes
- looking foolish
- and so forth

Their play is harmless and fun. As we get older, many of us begin to worry about all of these things, and we stop doing things that we think of as silly. This is a mistake. Being silly is not only enjoyable, it also can open up our creative channels. Allow some silliness into your life. You can easily incorporate one or more of the following activities into your daily life:

- make puns
- tell jokes
- recite limericks
- wear funny hats, on occasion
- spin around for no reason
- skip or jump on every available occasion
- fly a kite because you want to
- play a card game and make up the rules
- place something offbeat and unexpected in your office (I have a Lego telephone that works)

In other words, let your playful child come out of hiding and express itself. You become more open to possibilities when you can do things just for fun, be silly and not so concerned about appearing foolish. Your mind becomes more receptive, flexible, and adaptable. These are all positive characteristics that foster creativity.

Exercise 8.2: My Silly Side

Materials: Paper for writing or drawing. A writing instrument, or crayons, felt markers, or oil pastels

Directions: Imagine the following three situations, one at a time, and describe what you would do and/or feel. Write a description, or use the crayons, markers, or pastels to draw a symbolic representation of the feelings that come up for you.

You are playing a card game with a five-year-old; he knows the rules, but he does not want to use them for this game.

You go to an event where you do not know most people attending. Your supervisor or boss is present. The band plays a really up-tempo number and many people at the event flock to the dance floor, some without partners. They dance alone.

You are walking down the street and when you look around, you notice that the woman approaching you is skipping down the street.

Flexibility

Creating something new or novel involves mental flexibility. Flexibility is the ability to change, adapt, analyze, evaluate, and make reasoned judgments. Note that flexibility tempered with reason may be more advantageous than just being flexible, inasmuch as "bending with the wind" is not necessarily a positive characteristic.

The flexible person can:

● change routines and habits

● adapt to meet challenges

● analyze what is present to solve problems

● evaluate current functioning and possible alternatives

● judge the efficacy of the proposals and/or new creation

Changing routines and habits refers to the willingness to alter what one is doing in order to bring in some openness and a new perspective. New information promotes new ideas, but you have to adopt an attitude of receptivity and try alternative ways to create something new and original.

Adapting is making modifications to something already present, especially when that something is not working, or can be improved. The "something" presents you with a challenge, and you begin to explore ways of addressing the challenge, instead of ignoring it and maintaining the status quo.

Analysis is a process of thinking about the problem, challenge, process, or thing. It involves breaking the problem down into its components, understanding how these components are interrelated and interact, and what applications can be made of this information. Every invention involves analysis throughout its development. Creating new processes and procedures involves analysis, as does the creation of new products.

Evaluation of functioning, possibilities, alternatives, and the like is necessary to decide what to do or what not to do, what to keep and what to discard, what to add and what to subtract, and so forth. Evaluating the positive and negative aspects, the utility, and contributions of the various parts allows a more accurate assessment of the goodness and rightness of what is produced, or is being considered.

Judging the efficacy of the proposal and the new creation usually involves decision making after careful consideration. The careful consideration involves analysis and evaluation, with judgment as the final step. Sorting through all of the information and coming to conclusions is a high level of mental activity.

Creativity involves work. There may be times when you seemingly create something with very little effort, but that is only an illusion. The work took place on a nonconscious level, and you went through all the processes described for flexibility. The work may have been done rapidly, but it was done.

Divergent Thinking

There is a popular phrase, "thinking outside the box," which applies to divergent thought. This concept begins with what is common, usual, and/or conventional "wisdom," and considers it in a new way. This kind of thinking "diverges" from the commonplace.

To engage in divergent thinking means that you are not part of the crowd, not joining in "group think," and not doing what the masses are thinking or doing. You are willing to go against the tide of the "group's" opinion and perspective. ("Group," here, means any collection of people in small groups, e.g., family, to larger groups, e.g., the community.) Divergent thinking also involves imagination, open-mindedness, and flexibility. It is thinking in a different way—outside the box.

The next two exercises give you an opportunity to explore your capacity for divergent thinking and can spark some creativity.

Exercise 8.4: Oranges

Materials: Sheet of paper and a writing instrument

Directions: An uncle gives you a boxcar of oranges worth a great deal of money if you can figure out how to capitalize on the gift. You have one month before the oranges arrive. Make a list of all the ways you think the oranges could be used. Try to have at least twenty different items on your list. To get you started here are two examples:

- an orange juice concession at a festival
- an offering of orange futures on the commodities exchange

Exercise 8.5: Color and Design

Materials: A pack of 3- x 5-inch index cards that are blank on one side, and a crayon, felt marker, or oil pastel in the color of your choice (pick only one color).

Directions: You have been hired to produce designs for a new company that specializes in one-of-a-kind designs for special occasions. They have a contract for an event that wants designs using only one color on a white background. They need at least thirty different designs. Using the color you picked, draw as many different designs as you can think of on the cards.

Expressing Your Creativity

Opportunities to express your creativity are all around you. You just have to become aware of possibilities, open your mind to wonder, and give it a try. The exercises in this book are creative ways to be self-reflective. There are other parts of your life that have possibilities for creativity. Examine everything you do, encounter, and contemplate for ways that you can be creative. To get you started, some examples follow:

- Modify a favorite recipe by adding or changing the ingredients
- Paint your own design on a decorative item to use in your home, e.g., a flowerpot
- Stencil a design on a door in your home
- Write a poem to or about someone you love
- Use items that you would ordinarily throw away in new and different ways

There are numerous ways in which your creative side can be nurtured. You must search for the way that meets your needs and is consistent with your personality. You can also try different things to see how they fit you. For example you could try writing some thing based on these suggestions:

- lyrics for a song

- an essay

- a poem

- a play

- directions for others to learn how to do something

- a recipe

You can use art as an expression and draw, paint, stencil, sculpt, mold, construct a collage, make decoupage, or use mixed media. Music as an expression of your creative self is also very versatile; you can write music, perform music, arrange a score, or develop a process for teaching a variety of instruments or voice. Movement is another medium for creative expression. Various kinds of dance and exercises for different conditions lend themselves to creative expression.

There is one final exercise relating to creativity to try. It's modeled after the book on 101 ways to use something, e.g., a dead cat.

Exercise 8.6: 101 Uses for Old Newspapers

Materials: Four sheets of paper and a writing instrument, *or* various pictures from magazines, a glue stick, scissors and a pack of 5- x 8-inch unlined index cards.

Directions: For this variation, use the paper and writing instrument. You are creating ideas for a book on 101 ways to use old newspapers. Number 1 through 25 on each sheet of paper. Quickly list all the uses you can think of for old newspapers. Imagine and visualize how old newspapers could be adapted or modified for various uses. To get you started, here are three examples:

- fireplace logs

- paper machè

- lining for the cat's litter box

For this second variation, use the art materials. Find pictures of items you think could be made by using old newspapers. Cut out the pictures and glue them on the index cards. The first card should be labeled, "101 Uses for Old Newspapers."

Chapter 9

Your Inspirational Self

The part of you that relates to the spiritual, the meaning and purpose in your life, is called the Inspirational Self. This is the part of you that cannot be adequately described in words. Many people equate spiritual with religion, but spirituality is more than religious belief and faith, and you can be spiritual without being religious. Religion, for many, is their spiritual "self," and if this is true for you, this discussion is intended to build on and expand that foundation. If religion is not your spiritual "self," the intent of this discussion is for you to better understand how to bring your awareness of your spirituality into your life. To counter the mind-set that holds spirituality and religion to be the same thing, the term Inspirational Self is used.

Your Inspirational Self can help you to:

- Feel connected to others and to the universe
- Guide you to establish meaning and purpose for your life
- Promote altruism
- Reduce feelings of alienation and isolation
- Sustain you through adversity and other troubles
- Allow you to remain true and faithful to your principles

Your Inspirational Self adds richness and direction to your life, your relationships, and your endeavors. These are valid reasons to pay some attention to becoming more aware of your Inspirational Self and strengthening it. Increasing your awareness begins with the following discussion that defines and describes some components of your Inspirational Self.

Connections

The psychological sense of well-being and happiness is related to the extent and quality of your connections to others and to the universe.

Loneliness and despair occur when these connections are weak or lacking. There seems to be a social need to connect to others, and a need to feel that one has a part, a role, or that one is of some importance in the universe. It is very discouraging to feel that you have no meaningful connections to others, and/or that you experience what is known as "existential despair." Existential despair is that condition where you feel that you have no place, role, or importance in the universe.

The feeling of lack of connectedness can result when you experience grief, loss, rejection, and failure. You may withdraw psychologically because of the hurt you experience or fear, and this can produce the feeling that you are alone. The loneliness can be agonizing. No amount of human contact seems adequate to do away with the loneliness and produce feelings of being connected when you feel so alone.

This is when your Inspirational Self can be helpful in reconnecting you to others and to the universe. Accepting that you do need these connections can help you begin to move toward reconnecting.

Now, examine your current connections.

- Who and what are you connected to at this point in your life?

- Who and what provide these connections, and are they satisfying?

- Do you feel adrift and not really connected to anyone or anything?

- What impact does loneliness have on your physical and psychological well-being?

If you do have connections, it is reaffirming to recognize them at this point; and, if you do not have connections, it is sobering to realize the lack.

Meaning and Purpose

The meaning and purpose for your life come from within you and are enhanced by your connections, relationships, and works. Meaning and purpose are not given or bestowed upon you, you must search them out and recognize their existence. That search can be within a religious faith, but it can also be found without embracing any particular religion. You determine what meaning and purpose your life has, and where to find the meaning and purpose. Faith, belief, and acceptance of a religion may enhance your Inspirational Self, provide you with guidance and support, and enrich many aspects of your life, but you still have to recognize and accept them as meaningful.

It seems that gaining meaning and purpose for life can come about in a variety of ways, such as the following:

- Doing good works

- Having satisfying relationships

- Working for a cause

- Practicing a faith

Some people find meaning and purpose in giving to others through their works. Some even make their works their lives, e.g., Martin Luther King Jr., Mother Teresa, and CEOs who give up well-paying positions to become school teachers. You probably have some of these people in your community.

Relationships also can be a source for gaining meaning and purpose in life as these are the connections everyone needs. The quality of your relationships plays a very important role in the meaning and purpose you find for your life. (See chapter 10 where the topic of relationships is discussed more fully.)

Working for a cause can add considerable meaning and purpose to what you do with your life. Numerous women and men devote their lives to causes. Causes arouse passion and you have to be careful to not become too enmeshed with a cause. However, feeling deeply about something and working to correct an injustice or wrong is very uplifting. People work for their causes because they believe in them and also because the cause provides meaning and purpose to their lives. Some causes that you might consider working for and adopting as yours are such as the following:

- Preventing child abuse

- Helping victims of domestic violence

- Working for fair treatment for the disabled

- Ensuring voting rights for all Americans

Faith provides meaning and purpose for many people as evidenced by the number of those who attend and support churches, who pray, and support faith-based activities, e.g., schools. Religious people have faith that there is meaning and purpose in the universe, and that such meaning and purpose is expressed in the tenets of their particular faith.

There are also people who are not members of an organized religious body, but who are religious because they believe that the universe provides meaning and purpose. Evidence is mounting that those people who have faith promote their physical, emotional, and psychological health by practicing it. We do not yet know how this works, we are only able to observe the outcomes as compared with those who do not have faith, or are skeptical.

Altruism

Altruism means giving to others without having any expectation of payback. Whatever is given is offered voluntarily and is freely given because that is what you want to do. You do not expect to receive gratitude, compensation, favors in return, admiration, acceptance, or anything else. What you give is without conditions.

Many people seem willing to give to others but only because they want to be recognized and/or rewarded in some way. For example, when you do a favor for someone, do you expect him/her to remember the favor and to do you a favor in return? Are you displeased when your favors are not returned? These are examples of common expectations.

Altruism also means being able to receive from others without feeling diminished, obligated, or inadequate. It is a transcending experience when you can accept what others give you and, at the same time, have no expectation that those others are expected, obliged, or responsible to take care of you and your needs. Yes, you may need the gift, but you do not demand or require that someone provide you with it. You are appreciative and can accept it. The key component is how you feel about it.

Reflect on some of your past experiences where you did provide for or give something to another person. Were you expecting any of the following:

- something in return

- recognition

- gratitude

- admiration

- a future favor

In other words, were there strings attached? Be as honest with yourself as possible. It takes some special self-understanding and effort to be truly altruistic. As you try to strengthen your Inspirational Self, you may want to try to become more altruistic. That is, to freely give to others and be able to receive from others. For example, you might want to do one of the following:

- Mentor a child

- Read to someone in a nursing home

- Volunteer in your community

- Work on a Habitat housing project

- Serve at a soup kitchen

- Give a mother of small children an occasional break by watching the children
- Contribute to the drives for school supplies held in many communities
- Volunteer to be a teacher's aide
- Join the Literacy Council and teach an adult to read

There are many opportunities to be useful. You also can give to those who are nearest and dearest to you with no expectation of anything other than a possible "thank-you," and not feel rejected or diminished when you do not get anything in return. Give because you want to, not because you have to.

Alienation and Isolation

Alienation is the feeling of not being connected to anything or anyone. You feel that you have no meaningful relationships and that no one cares for you. This sense of not being connected to anyone generally occurs when you are emotionally detached from others because you are feeling any or all of the following emotions:

- hurt
- rejected
- angry and frustrated
- despairing

This feeling of alienation is a way of protecting yourself from further suffering. On some level you have decided that getting close to others, or letting them get close to you, is detrimental to your well-being. You extend your hurt to people and the world around you.

People also become alienated from their connection to the universe, especially when faced with the seeming indifference of the universe. They question the intent and purpose of a universe that allows the following to exist:

- Pain and suffering
- Abuse of the weak
- Unfairness and injustice
- War
- Famine
- Disease
- Pestilence
- Violence

These people become alienated because they feel helpless to effect positive changes for either personal concerns or those of society.

Even when they are one of a crowd, their alienation causes them to feel isolated. Feeling isolated can lead to further withdrawal, destructive acts both against the self and others, and physical and emotional conditions of ill health. Some people recognize that they are feeling this way and try to reestablish connections only to find that there is something internal that keeps them from connecting.

Your Inspirational Self can lead you to reestablishing connections with other people and with the universe. The connections will be different from those you previously had, but the new connections can reduce feelings of being alienated and isolated. You can be guided to:

- forgiveness

- letting go

- your inner resources

- hopefulness

- a new sense of self-identity

- a deeper wisdom and understanding

Working Through Adversity

It is the rare person who has not faced some adversity in their lives. There are also those who experience chronic adversity that has little or no chance for resolution. Chronic adversity can be difficult or impossible to overcome, for example:

- poverty

- terminal illness

- severe disability, such as paralysis

- war

- racism

- chronic mental illness

- loss of ability, such as brain damage

There are other adverse circumstances that can cause you to question the meaning and purpose of your life such as:

- loss of employment

- death of a loved one

- severe physical and/or emotional illness

- inability to effect positive changes for yourself and/or your family

- unsatisfying relationships

- depression

- rejection

Fighting the adverse circumstances can provide some measure of relief, but it is much more helpful to work through them and emerge stronger and more confident about your place in the world. Working through adversity promotes a deeper understanding of yourself and constructive use or development of your inner resources.

Victor Frankl's book, *Man's Search for Meaning* (1959), describes how the extremely adverse situation of being confined in the concentration camps of Nazi Germany did not keep some people from holding onto their higher values, faith, and inner resources. These permitted them to survive, to help others, and to resist being dehumanized. Although these were extreme circumstances, these descriptions show us what is possible, and they can serve as a guide for facing adversity of lesser proportion, but which still plays a significant part in your life.

Personal Principles

Your personal principles are the ethics, morals, and values that determine your actions. When any of these are ignored or violated, you will most likely feel guilty and ashamed. You may criticize and blame other people for what you did, but the ultimate responsibility rests with you.

An important reason why personal principles are often violated is that they are only dimly understood. Dimly understood in the sense that they were not freely chosen, and were neither examined, nor evaluated. They were unconsciously incorporated or imposed by parents, the church, other people, or were never developed.

Ethics

Ethics are the principles of right and wrong behavior. Our laws are designed to reflect the nation's ethics for right and wrong behavior. The laws are constantly being revised and updated. New laws are enacted as we become more aware of the various shades of gray for right and wrong. Acts are not always clearly right or wrong.

On a more personal level, do you have a clear understanding of what you consider to be right and what you consider to be wrong? Do the people involved or the circumstances make a difference in your considerations? Is the same behavior expected of children and adults? This subject is much too complex to even begin to address in this book, but

it is important. It can be important for you to reflect on what you consider to be ethical and unethical behavior separate from any laws gov-
erning behavior. You will want to formulate or become more aware of
your own ethics.

Morals

Morals are the behaviors that are considered good or bad. In one
sense, morals are not as clear-cut as ethics are because personal perceptions of what is good and what is bad are so varied. Morality is also a
very complex subject that in no way can be addressed adequately here.

Religions establish and emphasize parameters for moral behavior,
and there are considerable differences among and between religions
and within religions. Furthermore, perceptions about morality change
over time. Some of the questions you can explore for better self-
understanding of your own morality are as follows:

- Does my behavior reflect my morals?
- What do I consider to be "bad" behavior?
- What do I consider to be "good" behavior?
- Did I freely choose these morals or did I unconsciously incor-
  porate them from external influences?
- How do I feel when I act "bad"?
- How do I feel when I act "good"?
- What morals do I want to guide my behavior?

Values

Values are even more complex and varied than ethics or morals,
i.e., there are more shades of gray. When compared to values, ethics
are almost black-and-white issues. Furthermore, values tend to form
themselves into a dynamic value system where priorities can change
with circumstances and the people who are involved.

Rokeach in his book, *Beliefs, Attitudes and Values* (1972), defines
values as "abstract ideals, positive or negative" (124) that describe one's
ideals about conduct and what Rokeach terms "terminal goals." Ideal
standards for behavior and conduct are applied to such concepts as
cleanliness, sincerity, justice, and respect. Ideal terminal goals are concepts such as happiness, freedom, salvation, and fame.

Values are also hierarchical. That is, some values are given more
prominence than others. For example, you may value loyalty over truth,
although both are values you hold. This hierarchy, the unconscious
nature of many of your values, and the dynamic nature of a given value

system govern your behavior. You act or behave in accord with your values, whether you are consciously doing so or not.

If you want to know what your values are, examine your behavior. You may consciously think that you hold certain values, but your actions may indicate otherwise. Let's apply this concept to some of your behaviors relative to the belief that you have too much empathy.

Exercise 9.1: Values

Materials: Sheet of paper and a writing instrument

Directions: Rank the following values with your highest value receiving a rank of 1. Be sure to read the entire list before ranking the items.

Value	Rank
Honesty	_____
Respect	_____
Compassion	_____
Sincerity	_____
Honor	_____
Truthfulness	_____
Sensitivity	_____
Tolerance	_____
Fairness	_____
Self-discipline	_____

You may value all of these characteristics and believe that you govern your behavior in accord with them. These are also the characteristics that you look for in others, and you can be constantly disappointed when other people do not seem to hold the same values you do. This can be especially true for the people with whom you interact whose emotions you "catch."

The next step is to reflect on your behavior much of the time and answer the following questions.

1. Do you tell "white lies"?

2. Do you show respect to children?

3. What's your opinion of or reaction to single mothers on welfare?

4. Do you make flattering comments to others to make them feel good, or to make them like you?

5. Have you sought revenge?

6. Do you always give your honest opinion?

7. Have you overlooked or ignored someone's emotional distress?

8. Do you have friends from different races/ethnic groups and/or religions?

9. If you were given an opportunity to go to the head of the line in front of others who are waiting, would you take it?

10. In what area of your life do you lack self-discipline?

The point of this activity is to start you to become more aware and self-reflective about your values. You may be acting inconsistently with your values when you allow yourself to "catch" others' emotions that manipulate you. This may be why you are troubled by having too much empathy; your values are being compromised. Building your Inspirational Self increases your awareness of your values, their relative importance for you, and helps you allow them to govern your behavior in a more constructive way.

Now that we have defined some of the concepts associated with the Inspirational Self, we turn to exercises and activities that can build this area of your life.

Exercise 9.2: Spiritual Self-Appraisal

Materials: Sheet of paper; crayons, felt markers, or oil pastels; writing instrument and ruler

Directions: You will draw a bar graph to indicate your satisfactions with some spiritual aspects of your life. Begin by drawing a graph like the model on the next page.

Write the following words for the twelve spaces at the bottom of the page: *hope, meaning, purpose, values, faith, positive view, feel forgiven, at peace, comfort with the idea of my death, worthwhile, commitment,* and *direction.*

Select a color to represent each word and draw the bar with that color. Indicate the amount of satisfaction you have for each concept in your life as it is now. For example, you may be very hopeful and would draw a bar to the 85th percentile, or you may not feel that you have much direction in your life at this time, and you are so dissatisfied that you would draw a bar to the 15th percentile. When you have finished, look at your graph and think of ways to increase your satisfaction with any concept that is at less than 50 percent on your graph.

How many of these twelve concepts are a satisfying part of your life? How many have you consciously thought about before reading this book? Are you by nature a self-reflective person? No one can prescribe how to increase your spiritual resources, this is an individualistic concern and you should choose what to do. Guidance can be sought from many sources like books, tapes, trusted people, and so forth. However,

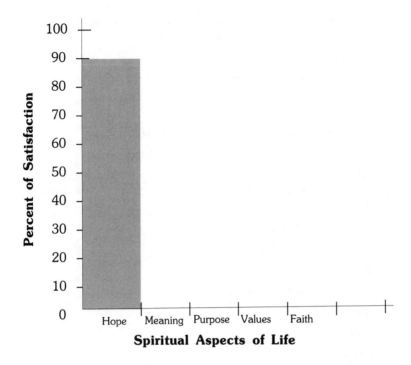

Spiritual Aspects of Life

the choices you make should be yours alone. Work on increasing your satisfaction for each of the concepts listed in your bar graph.

The next set of exercises are designed to provide some suggestions for increasing your satisfaction in these areas.

Exercise 9.3: Reflections on Your Inspirational Self

Materials: A notebook and writing instrument

Directions: Write a short essay on each of the following topics. Try to write at least one page for each. You may find that other images and memories emerge as you write and you will want to record these.

- A time when the purpose and meaning for your life was clear to you

- A time when you felt you had direction for your life

- What it feels like to not have meaning and purpose, or how it feels that the meaning and purpose are not clear to you

- Difficult choices you made and the consequences of these choices

- Encounter(s) with death or near death. This can be for you personally, or for someone near to you.
- Inspiring experiences

Read your essays and reflect on how these experiences have shaped you and your spiritual life.

Exercise 9.4: Making Space for Your Inspirational Self

Materials: A sheet of paper with a large circle drawn on it. Make the circle large enough to fit the page. Crayons, felt markers or oil pastels; a writing instrument

Directions: Within the circle draw symbols for the following:

- something that gives you hope
- your faith and its benefits
- affirmation and support
- respect
- trust
- enjoyment
- optimism
- your major commitments
- feelings of joy and connections
- overcoming adversity

You now have your spiritual development seal. Add any other symbols of spirituality that appeal to you.

If you do not know what you are looking for, you may not find it. Your Inspirational Self provides the richness of your existence and should not be ignored. There are so many ways to tap into a spiritual life that you can choose how you want to access it. One way that has not yet been discussed is known by a variety of terms:

- becoming still
- meditation
- prayer
- vows of silence

Whatever term appeals to you can suggest how you want to proceed. All are solitary and quiet methods that do not involve either thought or emotions. You do not think, talk, or need to label your feelings. You are instructed just to stay in the moment and breathe.

There are numerous guides to these practices and all involve the following:

- a quiet place

- freedom from distractions

- sitting or kneeling

- concentrating on your breath and breathing

- giving up control of your thoughts

- becoming peaceful

Prayer can involve speaking aloud, but many people pray silently and open themselves for all the spirit of the Supreme Being to enter them. This process is similar in many respects to others, e.g., meditation.

Exercise 9.5: Finding Your Way

Directions: Find a quiet place that is free of distractions where you can sit or kneel in comfort. Wear loose clothing or loosen your clothes. Many people find it helpful to close their eyes, but you can keep your eyes open if you choose.

Begin by sitting silently with your eyes open or closed. Pay attention to your breathing and consciously allow it to become deep and even. If thoughts of other matters intrude, bring your attention back to your breath. Do this for as long as you can. Be patient. You may find yourself easily distracted at first, but with practice you will be able to be still for longer periods of time.

When you open your eyes and/or bring your awareness back to the room, pay attention to the following:

- how your body feels

- sounds

- aromas

- objects in the room

- your emotional state or what you are feeling

Do not try to evaluate what you did or what you experienced. Just accept it.

Variations: If you prefer to pray, notice the same things after praying, as listed above.

There are classes that can teach you how to meditate or relax. Either way you choose, you can learn to find your own way to your Inspirational Self.

One last thought and exercise. Part of your spiritual journey may involve letting go of negative experiences that sap your energy. These are the experiences that continue to trouble you, for example:

- emotional and/or physical abuse

- hurt

- rejection

- demeaning and devaluing comments

- jealousy

- envy

These negative experiences may be a part of your unfinished business and may have been troubling you for a very long time. It is now time to let go of the feelings around these experiences as you cannot change them or make them better; they serve only to keep you from realizing your potential as a fully functioning adult. Letting go does not mean that you must forget. But it does involve a certain measure of forgiveness, for others and for yourself. The following exercise is a start for letting go of your negative experiences.

Exercise 9.6: Letting Go of Negative Experiences

Materials: A box or other container that can be discarded. Strips of paper and a writing instrument

Directions: Recall as many of your negative experiences with people who hurt you as you can and describe them on separate strips of paper. Put the strips in the box or container. Then, dispose of the container and strips by:

- Burning them

- Taking them to the dump and leaving them there

- Putting them in the trash for pick up

- Tearing the strips and letting the wind take them away.(Yes, I know this is littering but doing it once can be forgiven.)

When you dispose of the strips, repeat to yourself, "I am letting go of these negative experiences. I am forgiving others and myself. I am growing and developing."

Chapter 10

Better Relationships

This chapter brings together the different topics previously discussed for applications to your relationships. It describes a technique for empathic responding that does not require you to "catch" the other person's emotions. It seemed both necessary and more helpful to explain first how and why you "catch" emotions, the short-term protection of emotional shielding, and how to develop some components of the self before addressing the topics in this chapter. This sequence provided you with some basic information and understanding about:

- The faulty assumptions that may be directing your attitudes and behavior

- The characteristics of "senders"

- The unconscious incorporation of others' emotions, and some possible reasons that allow you to receive these emotions

- Some techniques for building emotional shielding against external and internal forces

- Some descriptions and exercises for further developing some aspects of your self

- The importance of strong and resilient boundaries

Your understanding and personal development of these topics are important for you to be able to maintain an appropriate level of empathy, and not become enmeshed or overwhelmed by others' emotions. It was said earlier in the book that being empathic is one of the positive characteristics of healthy adult narcissism. For that reason, you do not want to move toward becoming unempathic. Your goal is to be appropriately empathic.

Empathy

The discussion now turns to *empathy,* which is defined here as voluntarily entering the world of the other person, feeling what he/she is experiencing without losing your sense of self, and reacting or communicating that understanding to the other person. The key words here are:

● voluntarily

● feeling

● without losing

● understanding

In this definition for empathy, you do not involuntarily "catch" the other person's feelings. Instead, you *voluntarily* make a conscious decision to empathize. There will still be times when you will find that you begin to empathize unconsciously, but because you have begun to take charge of your emotional life, you will, in most instances, make your own decision to empathize—or not to empathize. It will not be forced on you by senders and others' projections.

The feelings that you sense and experience in true empathy do not enmesh or overwhelm you. You do feel the other person's feelings, such as:

● despair

● yearning and longing

● pain and misery

● powerlessness

● anger and rage

● anguish

But you will not be taken over, manipulated, and/or destroyed by the other person's feelings. You do not want to give up this ability to tune into others, as it fosters meaningful connections. For example, gifted therapists are able to use this characteristic to help their clients; it is one of their most valuable tools. Almost *everyone* is drawn to and appreciates someone who knows, at a deep level, what they are feeling and going through, and you want to keep your ability to do so.

A critical component for true empathy is to not lose your sense of *self* during the experiencing of the other person's feelings. This is your control mechanism that prevents you from being taken over, manipulated, and/or destroyed by the other person's feelings. This critical component is the focus of much of what has been presented throughout this book. You need a strong sense of where "you" end; i.e., the extension of your self, and where the other person begins. You also need to develop an acute awareness of what you are feeling and thinking, so that you can pull back when you are in danger of becoming enmeshed or overwhelmed.

The conditions and circumstances that can lead to "catching" others' emotions are these:

- A lack of strong and resilient boundaries

- Your faulty assumptions about the limits of your responsibility

- Your nonverbal behaviors of rapport

- Your psychological investment in the well-being of the other person

- The developmental level of your psychological self

It is now time for you to take control of your self and decide the degree and extent of your empathy. As someone who is emotionally susceptible, it is also important for you to understand that, although you are feeling what the other person feels, that kind of empathy is more like what a baby or child experiences because they have no psychological boundaries, or very weak boundaries. Babies and children are very open to "catching" others' emotions, especially those of the mother. What you are working to develop now that should have developed earlier in your life is the kind of empathy that leaves you:

- In control

- Retaining your sense of your Self

- In no danger of being manipulated

- Not at risk of getting lost

- Not fearful of destruction

- Able to fortify your relationships

This kind of empathy is appropriate and healthy adult empathy

Empathic Responding

It takes time and effort to build your self to this point, so be patient. You also want to retain and/or improve the quality of your important relationships, and so you do not want to become insensitive or uncaring. What follows here are suggestions for how you can use empathic responding, but not "be" empathic, i.e., not enter the world of the other person. Empathic responding for this discussion has the following characteristics:

- You are detached from the other person's emotional intensity.

- Thinking is used instead of your feelings.

- You consciously and unconsciously block projections from other people.

- You are consciously aware of your feelings at that time.

- Your emotional shielding is in place.

This type of responding allows you to identify and acknowledge what the other person is saying, meaning, and feeling *without* you having to join in with the feeling or lose your sense of self.

Responding empathically can be very effective because the other person feels heard and understood. That's a primary benefit for empathy, and a more detached empathic responding can produce similar results without having a negative impact on you. Furthermore, you will find it easier to recognize when others are trying to manipulate you, and be better able to resist.

The Nonverbal Stance

Learning how to respond empathically begins with using the nonverbal behaviors that were described in the section on emotional shielding from external forces in chapter 4.

To summarize those suggestions:

- Do not initiate or maintain eye contact.

- Create and maintain a slightly larger personal zone.

- Orient your body away from the other person.

- Keep your primary focus on the words used by the other person.

- Tune in to your emotional experiencing and suppress it for the time being.

By following these instructions, you will remove yourself from the emotional intensity of the other person, establish your own separateness, shield yourself against projections, while, at the same time, you listen to what the person is saying and feeling.

Listen for Content

The next step is to listen to what is said for the most important content. That is, what is most important for that person. You are thinking, analyzing, and forming conclusions as the other person speaks, as listening is faster than speaking. Hear both the spoken and unspoken messages. That will give you time to decide if the unspoken message is an attempt to manipulate you. At this point, listening also can include asking questions. Do not assume you understand what the other person means, or if you do understand, also ask questions anyway to check out your understanding. Ask questions like these:

- You said _____ , what do you mean?

- Did, or do you mean _____ ?

- What exactly are you asking of me?

- I'm not sure I understand, could you explain that further?

If you do not want to ask questions, or if you feel that what was said was pretty clear, you can move to the next step, that of paraphrasing what the person said.

Paraphrasing

When you *paraphrase* you repeat the essence of what was said, but use different words. Paraphrasing is helpful in two-way communication because there are always times when people do not say what they mean to say, or when what they said was not accurately heard.

Paraphrasing will give the other person an opportunity to correct what was meant, or what was heard. Note that it is important to use different words when paraphrasing, so the other person does not think you are parroting or mocking him/her. Following are three examples of paraphrasing, and three statements for you to try to paraphrase.

Exercise 10.1: Paraphrasing

Directions: First read the examples and then try to paraphrase the next three statements.

Examples

1. **Statement:** "This headache is driving me crazy." **Paraphrase:** "You are really hurting."

2. **Statement:** "Why haven't you called me more often?" **Paraphrase:** "I haven't called as often as you expected me to."

3. **Statement:** "It's hard to get up in the morning since I don't have anything I have to do." **Paraphrase:** "You're sleeping in most mornings."

Statements	**Your Paraphrases**
1. I'm feeling really down.	1. _____
2. Nothing ever goes right for me.	2. _____
3. I wish I could be happy.	3. _____

When Not to Paraphrase

There are situations where you do not need to paraphrase, and above all, you do not want be empathic. You will want to refrain from paraphrasing when someone makes blaming, criticizing, demeaning, and devaluing comments whether the comments are about you or about someone else. You can try to not respond to these comments, but if that is impossible (e.g., you cannot ignore a parent because that's not a part of your personality), it is still best not to paraphrase.

For example, comments such as these should never be paraphrased:

- You look a mess.

- Why can't you do anything right?

- I'd think you would be ashamed to be seen like this.

- Can't you do something about your weight?

- You ought to be more sensitive (thoughtful, like a sibling, etc.).

These are the types of comments that it is best to ignore, deflect, change the topic, or ask an unrelated question. If all these fail, you should leave. You do not have to open yourself to being manipulated by the guilt or shame that can be induced if you continue to participate in any interaction that puts you down. It is helpful if you do not become defensive, e.g., try to explain, as that is perceived as a weakness, or to go on the offensive, as that makes matters worse.

Nearly Empathic

Once you feel comfortable with paraphrasing or choosing not to paraphrase, you are ready to try empathic responding. To do this, you add to the content of the message the underlying feelings that you *think* the person is experiencing. Stay with your thought processes. Be very clear in your mind that you are not trying to feel what that person is experiencing, you are only trying to analyze what was said to determine what the feeling(s) could be. You can even phrase your response somewhat tentatively as a question.

Let's return to the statements in exercise 10.1 and list some possible feelings that are not being directly expressed.

Statement	Possible Feelings
This headache is driving me crazy.	Annoyance, frustration, inadequacy
Why haven't you called me more often?	Rejected, blaming others, lonely, hurt
It's hard to get up in the morning since I don't have anything I have to do.	Lonely, depressed, dejected, adrift, alienated
I'm feeling really down.	Lonely, alienated, despair, inept, angry, inadequate, helpless, hopeless
Nothing ever goes right for me.	Inadequate, incompetent, helpless, hopeless
I wish I could be happy.	Ineffective, depressed, alienated, unhappy.

There are many possible feelings for each statement. What you could do is to ask the person, "Are you feeling _____?" It may be obvious from what is said what the person is feeling, especially if you know him/her well, but asking the question protects you from joining in with the feeling. Another protective statement and question response is, "I'm not sure I understand. Could you tell me more about it."

Responding to Manipulative Statements

Once you realize that the other person is trying to control or manipulate you, you have several choices for responding. You may do any of these:

- say nothing
- agree to be controlled or manipulated
- become defensive
- attack or go on the offensive
- assert your separateness and individuality

Ignoring and/or withdrawing by saying nothing is a response that can be effective for protecting yourself. These responses remove you from the situation. Becoming defensive is counterproductive as that gives the other person a wedge for getting you to do what he/she wants you to do.

Attacking and going on the offensive as responses can be effective. However, in some cases, because of the nature of the relationship, you may find that a counterattack overwhelms you and leaves you in a worse position. The most effective and satisfying response is one that asserts your separateness and individuality, serves notice that you are aware of the attempts to manipulate you, and that you will determine what you will or will not do.

There are occasions where any of the other responses will be effective and you will want to remember them and retain them as possible responses. For example, rather than becoming enmeshed or overwhelmed, you can withdraw.

How can you assert your independence without destroying the relationship? That is, how can you refuse to be controlled and/or manipulated and still make an empathic response? There are effective strategies, many of which are discussed in this book. For example, you can do the following:

- Become aware of and then deal with your faulty assumptions

- Develop emotional shielding against internal and external forces

- Fortify your boundaries to be stronger and more resilient

- Grow and develop your underdeveloped narcissism

- Use nonverbal behavior to protect against projections and "catching" emotions

- Practice being verbally assertive

Verbal Assertiveness

Five verbal strategies for assertiveness are presented below. These are only some of the many assertive strategies that are possibilities, and are used as examples to get you started thinking about some that fit your personality. Each is briefly discussed and illustrated.

The five strategies are these:

- Pick one piece

- Play stupid/distracted

- Reinforce the positive

- Refuse to "read minds"

- Ask for honesty and directness

Pick one piece refers to responding only to a part of the message, usually the least important part. For example, when someone says, "If you cared," as the lead-in to a manipulation, your verbal response might be:

- "I do care but not to that extent."

- "What do you mean by 'if'?"

- "Caring to you seems to mean doing what you want."

- "Caring means different things to each of us."

Any of these responses would convey the clear message that you understand what the other person is trying to do.

Playing stupid or distracted can also be an effective strategy, although it could be said that this is not assertive behavior. It's a kind of withdrawal. For this strategy you deliberately misunderstand the message and your response is off target. Using the previous example, the play stupid or distracted response would be something like:

- "Isn't it terrible when no one cares."

- "I can't get anyone to do what I want them to do either."

- "You care so much about everyone."

There are numerous such responses.

Reinforcing the positive means selecting some part of the manipulative statement that could be interpreted as positive, and then reinforcing it. For example, when someone says, "If you cared you would _____ ," you could reinforce the caring part by responding that you do care and you show it when you _____ _____ (fill in the blank). Or, you could describe what caring means to you. Or, you could point out how the other person demonstrates caring.

Refuse to read minds refers to making a verbal statement that the other person seems to expect you to know what he/she wants or needs without that person having to say so, and you do not want to do that. This strategy calls for a great deal of assertiveness on your part as you will have to say, "I cannot or will not try to read your mind." For example, when someone says, "If you cared you'd know what I wanted (needed, meant)," your assertive response could be, "I gave up trying to read minds, since I am wrong so often, but that doesn't mean I don't care. Help me understand exactly what it is you are asking of me."

The last verbal strategy is pretty clear. You simply ask the person to be direct and honest instead of indirectly asking you to do something. Use statements like, "I would really appreciate you being upfront with me and saying what you want." If you want to be emphatic you could add, "in words of two syllables or less." A question similar to, "What do you really want?" is also effective.

Standing your ground and insisting that the person be direct and honest will not be easy because the person who is manipulative and/or controlling does not like to be challenged in any way. This person may try to make you feel inept, stupid, crazy, etc., but do not give in. Say, "It would waste less time if you would be more direct, and there is less chance of misunderstanding." Block off any feelings of guilt or shame that might be triggered. You can deal with these later when you are alone. Stay with your thought processes when you are with this person.

Exercise 10.2: Verbal Strategies

Materials: Sheet of paper and a writing instrument

Directions: Give a response to each of the following remarks that would be a verbal strategy, e.g., that would reinforce the positive. Choose any strategy you wish. Pretend that someone close to you made the remark and is trying to manipulate or control you.

1. Don't you want to please me?

2. I want/need you to (do something you do not want to do).

3. Don't worry about me.

4. You should have known or understood what I needed.

5. You ought to be more sensitive.

6. Why can't you be thoughtful, like your sister is?

The Realistic Ideal State

It will take you some time to get to the point where you can allow yourself to be empathic and not fear enmeshment or being overwhelmed. It can be a slow process, but you must continue to work at it and celebrate every bit of progress you make. How can you know when you've arrived? Some of the following internal states, attitudes, and behaviors will be clues that will let you know how much progress you have achieved:

- There is mutual respect in your relationships.
- You do not seek power and control, and are able to recognize and resist those that do.
- You care for others but are careful not to exploit them or to allow yourself to be exploited.
- You care for yourself, flaws and all.
- You want caring, attention and admiration from some people, but do not need it.

● You are independent and interrelated with others.

● You have a firm idea of the limits of your personal responsibility.

● You can say no, mean it, and not have guilty feelings, or at least you can manage the guilt.

My Hope for You

I wish you well in all of your future endeavors and relationships. Taking steps to reduce your emotional susceptibility, build and fortify your boundaries, become more separated and individuated, and developing your healthy adult narcissism can lead you to realizing your potential as an independent person who is also interdependent. You can forge strong and meaningful connections to others without losing your "self" and will be able to withstand attempts by others to enmesh, manipulate, or overwhelm you. You will have appropriate empathy rather than feeling overempathic. My hope is that you will accomplish all of these.

References

Brown, N. 2001. *Children of the Self-Absorbed*. Oakland, CA: New Harbinger Publications.

―――. 1998. *The Destructive Narcissistic Pattern*. Westport, CN: Praeger.

Brown, N. 1992. Comparison of described empathic and nominated empathic individuals. *Psychological Reports*. 64:27–32.

Ellis, A. 1973. *Humanistic Psychotherapy: The Rational-Emotive Approach*. New York: McGraw-Hill.

Frankl, V. E. 1959. *Man's Search for Meaning: An Introduction to Logotherapy*. Boston: Beacon Press.

Hall, E. 1959. *The Silent Language*. New York: Facett.

Hatfield, E., J. Cacioppo, and R. Rapson. 1994. *Emotional Contagion*. New York: Cambridge University Press.

Kernberg, O. 1990. *Borderline Conditions and Pathological Narcissism*. Northvale, NJ: Jason Aronson, Inc.

Klein, M. 1952. The origins of transference. In *Envy and Gratitude and Other Works 1946–1963*. New York: Delta Books.

Kohut, H. 1977. *The Restoration of the Self*. New York: International Universities Press.

Mahler, M., F. Pine, and A. Bergman. 1975. *The Psychological Birth of the Human Infant*. New York: Basic Books.

O'Neill, M. S., and C. E. Newbolt. 1994. *Boundary Power*. Antioch, TN: Sonlight Publishing Co.

Rogers. C. 1975. Empathic: An unappreciated way of being. *The Counseling Psychologist*. 5(2):2-9.

Rokeach, M. 1972. *Beliefs, Attitudes and Values.* San Francisco: Jossey-Bass.

Other Works Consulted

Greenberg, L., and S. Paivio. 1997. *Working with Emotions in Psychotherapy.* New York: The Guilford Press.

Shostrom, E. 1972. *Freedom to Be.* New York: Prentice-Hall.

Some Other
New Harbinger Titles

The 50 Best Ways to Simplify Your Life, Item FWSL $11.95

When Anger Hurts Your Relationship, Item WARY $13.95

The Couple's Survival Workbook, Item CPSU $18.95

Loving Your Teenage Daughter, Item LYTD $14.95

The Hidden Feeling of Motherhood, Item HFM $14.95

Parenting Well When Your Depressed, Item PWWY $17.95

Thinking Pregnant, Item TKPG $13.95

Pregnancy Stories, Item PS $14.95

The Co-Parenting Survival Guide, Item CPSG $14.95

Family Guide to Emotional Wellness, Item FGEW $24.95

How to Survive and Thrive in an Empty Nest, Item NEST $13.95

Children of the Self-Absorbed, Item CSAB $14.95

The Adoption Reunion Survival Guide, Item ARSG $13.95

Undefended Love, Item UNLO $13.95

Why Can't I Be the Parent I Want to Be?, Item PRNT $12.95

Kid Cooperation, Item COOP $14.95

Breathing Room: Creating Space to Be a Couple, Item BR $14.95

Why Children Misbehave and What to do About it, Item BEHV $14.95

Couple Skills, Item SKIL $15.95

The Power of Two, Item PWR $15.95

The Queer Parent's Primer, Item QPPM $14.95

Illuminating the Heart, Item LUM $13.95

Dr. Carl Robinson's Basic Baby Care, Item DRR $10.95

The Ten Things Every Parent Needs to Know, Item KNOW $12.95

Call **toll free, 1-800-748-6273,** or log on to our online bookstore at **www.newharbinger.com** to order. Have your Visa or Mastercard number ready. Or send a check for the titles you want to New Harbinger Publications, Inc., 5674 Shattuck Ave., Oakland, CA 94609. Include $4.50 for the first book and 75¢ for each additional book, to cover shipping and handling. (California residents please include appropriate sales tax.) Allow two to five weeks for delivery.

Prices subject to change without notice.